Table of Contents

RUDE
FRENCH

ALTERNATIVE FRENCH PHRASEBOOK

by
Georges Pilard

This second edition published
by Chambers Harrap Publishers Ltd 2007
7 Hopetoun Crescent
Edinburgh EH7 4AY
Great Britain

Previous edition published 2002

ISBN 978 0245 60784 4

Designed and typeset by Chambers Harrap Publishers Ltd,
Edinburgh
Printed in Great Britain by Clays Ltd, St Ives plc

Contributors

Editor
Georges Pilard

Translations
Anna Stevenson
Kate Nicholson

Illustrations
Glen McBeth

Publishing Manager
Anna Stevenson

Prepress Controller
Heather Macpherson

Introduction

It is a significant fact that the first thing many people do when leafing through a dictionary is to find the rude words, and sometimes write to the publisher to complain about their very presence in the book. For slang seems to scandalize and to fascinate people in equal measure. It is often regarded as a freaky offshoot of language: a repellent but endlessly fascinating monster. But to consider it as nothing more than the language of filth and vulgarity is to misunderstand its nature.

Victor Hugo once called it "a language of combat" as it was born primarily out of the experience of the poor, the disenfranchised and the rebellious. There is no denying that it is the language of aggression, mockery and scorn. But its saving grace is its humour – after all laughter is a well-known defence mechanism in times of hardship – as well as its refreshing candour.

With this new, updated edition of *Rude French*, complete with great new illustrations and improved presentation, we will no doubt demonstrate once again that French slang is more than just a collection of coarse and unpleasant words and expressions, and show what an immensely robust, colourful and expressive language it can be.

The aim of this new little volume is therefore to explore French slang and celebrate its richness, to inform as well as to entertain.

It was designed as an alternative phrasebook and as such it covers most situations that a traveller might encounter on a trip to France. However its approach is resolutely unprudish, and the canons of good taste and political correctness are never allowed to get in the way of authenticity and fun.

In addition to thematic chapters complete with numerous examples and humorous illustrations, *Rude French* contains some enlightening information about the history of slang and its place in literature, as well as jokes and word games.

Finally, an extended, fully illustrated section on gestures will help you understand some of the nuances of French body language.

May we wish you a pleasant journey through the seamier side of the French language.

accommodation

As a Briton staying in a French hotel you might find yourself lying awake at night trying to figure out how hotel proprietors in France manage to make a decent living while charging only half what their British counterparts do. Chances are you'll fall asleep before finding a satisfactory explanation. Just in case your slumber is interrupted by a dripping tap, the occasional bedbug, or the furious creaking in the room next door, we've decided to include a chapter to help you communicate effectively with any French Basil Fawlty.

A few useful phrases in context

A place to suit your budget

On est descendu dans un hôtel super classe avec câble, mini-bar, jacuzzi, sauna, tennis, salle de billard, la totale quoi. Y'avait même des plumards dans la piaule!
We stayed in a dead classy hotel with cable TV, mini-bar, jacuzzi, sauna, tennis courts, pool room, the works. There were even beds in the room!

L'hôtel payait pas de mine, mais il était nickel, hyper calme, et le petit déj impec, avec kawa à volonté. La femme de ménage est même venue me faire un gros câlin gratos.
The hotel might not have looked it, but it was spotless, dead quiet, and it served a top breakfast with as much coffee as you could drink. The cleaning lady even came and "warmed the bed" free of charge.

Ils ont passé la nuit à se faire bouffer par les puces, à se boucher le nez, et à écouter les autre clients graillonner pour un prix tout à fait raisonnable.
They spent the whole night getting eaten alive by the fleas, having to hold their noses for the smell and listening to the other guests hawking up phlegm, all for a very reasonable price.

Il est pas cool le taulier: il a menacé de lâcher ses clébards si on n'avait pas décarré de la piaule d'ici midi!
The hotel manager's none too laid-back; he threatened to let his dogs loose on us if we weren't out of the room by midday.

We're not satisfied until you are

Dans la turne, ils avaient mis un écriteau qui disait qu'ils acceptaient pas les animaux. Sûrement parce qu'avec les punaises, les morbacs et les cafards, ils avaient déjà une sacrée ménagerie.
They'd put a sign in the room saying that pets weren't allowed. Probably because what with the bedbugs, the lice and the cockroaches, they were already running a bloody zoo.

Vous vous foutez de la gueule du monde: vous nous avez refilé une piaule avec vue imprenable sur les cuisines, des poils de diverses provenances incrustés dans le baveux et des draps avec tellement de cartes de France dessus qu'on dirait un atlas.
You really are taking the piss: you've given us a room that looks straight onto the kitchens, there's hairs from God-knows-where embedded in the soap and the sheet has that many maps of France on it you'd think it's an atlas.

La personne qui l'avait précédé dans la piaule devait être bien nourrie, comme en témoignait la présence dans les chiottes d'un colombin géant et rebelle.
Whoever had had the room before him must have been well-fed, judging by the huge floater in the bog.

More hotel misery

Le pire truc qui puisse t'arriver quand tu voyages seul et que t'as un coup de blues, c'est d'entendre un couple en train de baiser dans la piaule d'à côté alors que t'essayes de pioncer.
The worst thing when you're travelling alone and you're feeling a bit down is to have to listen to the couple in the room next door shagging when you're trying to get some sleep.

Comme la chaudière de l'hôtel était HS elle s'est rincée avec de la flotte glacée, après quoi elle s'est frictionnée avec une serviette plus que douteuse que le taulier avait fauchée dans un hôtel parisien.
As the boiler in the hotel was knackered, she rinsed herself in freezing water, then rubbed herself down with a very dodgy towel which the owner had nicked from a hotel in Paris.

Si on se faisait une partie de cartes? De toutes façons, on fermera pas l'œil de la nuit: sans la clime on crève de chaleur et avec la clime impossible de pioncer, tellement elle fait de boucan.
Fancy a game of cards? After all, we're not going to get any shuteye all night; without the air conditioning on we'll die of the heat and if we turn it on we'll never get to sleep for the racket.

Vu comme Jeannot l'avait riquiqui au sortir de la douche, Fred jugea inutile de lui demander s'il restait de l'eau chaude.
Given that Jeannot was suffering from a slight shrinkage problem when he came out of the shower, Fred decided there was no point asking him if there was any hot water left.

Je me suis pris une sacrée châtaigne en allumant la loupiote pour faire la chasse aux cafards.

I got a hell of an electric shock when I switched the lamp on to chase away the cockroaches.

Expecting the unexpected

Tu sais, les allées et venues continuelles dans les couloirs, les lourdes qu'ont claqué toute la nuit, le miroir au-desssus du paddock, tout ça c'est lié. On a mal compris, le mec de l'office du tourisme, il nous a pas dit que c'était un ancien hôtel particulier, il nous a dit "c'est un hôtel un peu particulier". Nuance!

You know, the continual comings and goings in the corridors, the doors slamming all night, the mirror on the ceiling above the bed, it's all connected. We misunderstood the guy in the tourist office – he didn't say it was a boarding house, he said a it was a bawdy house. Not quite the same thing!

Le leader du groupe de rock est gentiment venu s'excuser d'avoir saccagé notre chambre; il nous a dit que, lui et ses potes étant rentrés bourrés, ils s'étaient gourrés de piaule, d'où le bordel innommable qui y régnait.

The leader of the rock band came and very politely apologized to us for having wrecked our room; he told us that he and his mates had come home plastered and had wandered into the wrong room – hence the godawful shambles.

Le touriste avait appelé les flics parce que toutes les cinq minutes des clients de l'hôtel débarquaient dans sa piaule et venaient se bâcher dans son paddock avec lui et sa bonne femme: y'avait de l'abus! A l'autre bout du fil le flic se marrait: sans le savoir le touriste en pétard était descendu à L'Échangeur, la fameuse boîte à partouzes.

The tourist had called the cops because every five minutes hotel guests were turning up in his room and crashing out in his bed beside him and his missus: it was a bit much! On the other end of the phone the cop was killing himself laughing; the fuming tourist had unwittingly gone to stay at The Interchange, the famous hotel for swingers.

Je suis descendu prendre mon petit déj en calbute parce que mon unique falzar était resté coincé dans la machine à repasser.

I had to come down for breakfast in my boxers coz my only pair of strides had got stuck in the trouser press.

air-conditioning: la clime
bed: le paddock, le pageot, le pieu, le plumard, le pucier
bedsheets: les bâches *(fem.)*
blanket: la couvrante
breakfast: le petit déj
clean: nickel
coffee: le kawa, le jus, le petit noir
dirty: crade, cradingue, crado, craspec, dégueulasse
door: la lourde
electric current: le jus
expensive: chéro; *to be expensive*: coûter bonbon, coûter la peau des fesses
go to bed (to): se bâcher, se zoner, se pieuter
hotel proprietor: le taulier, le marchand de sommeil
hotel thief: le rat d'hôtel
lamp: la loupiote
maid: la bon(n)iche
noise: le boucan, le barouf, le chambard, le potin, le ramdam
out of order: en rade
oversleep (to): avoir une panne d'oreiller
room: la piaule, la carrée, la turne
sleep (to): pioncer, roupiller, en écraser
smell (to): refouler, trouilloter, coincer, schlinguer, fouetter, cocoter
soap: le baveux
suitcase: la valoche
tacky: ringard
telephone: le bigophone
television: la téloche
toilet: les chiottes *(masc.)*, les goguenots *(masc.)*, les gogues *(masc.)*
toilet paper: le papier cul, le PQ
uncomfortable: *(of bed, armchair)* rembourré avec des noyaux de pêche
water: la flotte

Did you know that

The word *goguenots* (often abbreviated to
"gogues"), meaning "toilet", comes from a
Normandy dialectal word meaning
"cider pot".

Test your rude French

Try and match the sentence in French with its accurate English
translation.

❶ **Elle ouvrit les rideaux de sa piaule et vit un mec en train de
montrer sa boutique de l'autre côté de la rue**
a) She opened her bedroom curtains and saw a guy exposing himself
on the other side of the street
b) She opened her bedroom curtains and saw a proud shopkeeper
showing customers round his establishment across the road
c) She opened her bedroom curtains and saw a window-dresser at
work in the shop across the road

❷ **Je me suis pété la gueule en essayant de ramasser le baveux**
a) I went to the local bar-cum-newsagent to buy a newspaper and
ended up getting pissed
b) I fell down trying to pick up the soap
c) I tried to score, without success

❸ **J'ai pas pu fermer l'œil de la nuit à cause de la gonzesse de
la piaule d'à côté qui s'est envoyée en l'air toute la nuit avec
son petit copain**
a) I couldn't sleep a wink because the little girl next door and her
friend played trampoline on the bed all night long
b) I couldn't sleep a wink because the couple in the room next to
mine were on a very noisy acid trip all night
c) I couldn't sleep a wink because the couple in the room next to
mine were at it all night

RUDE drinking

Britain and France have very different drinking "cultures". The puddles of vomit that adorn many a British pavement on weekend nights are largely absent from French streets, public drunkenness and pub brawls are a rarity and you will find few black-clad bouncers standing at the door of French cafés. But fret not! There is still plenty of scope to consume vast quantities of alcohol south of Cap Gris-Nez: starting with "l'apéro", followed by plenty of wine during your meal and one or several postprandial brandies to wrap it all up. And why not make your cup of coffee more interesting by adding a drop or two of Calvados?

A few useful phrases in context

What's your poison?

Sa caisse marche au sans plomb et lui il carbure au whisky.
His car runs on unleaded and he runs on whisky.

Il s'est envoyé quatre pastis avant le repas, deux bouteilles de rouquin pendant, et trois poires après; il a appris à se modérer.
He knocked back four glasses of pastis before the meal, two bottles of red wine during, and three pear brandies after; he's learned to restrain himself.

Tu nous remets deux mousses sans faux-col, Dédé? Et un paquet de goldos aussi, tu seras gentil!
Can we get another two beers without the froth on the top, Dédé? And a packet of Gauloises too, if you don't mind.

Scenes of bar life

Au fond du bistrot, un type genre blouson noir massacrait le flip, pendant que sa gonzesse sirotait un panaché en écoutant une rengaine au juke-box.
At the back of the bar this biker guy was making mincemeat of the pinball machine, while his bird was sipping a shandy and listening to a tune on the jukebox.

Comment ça, je bois trop? C'est que mon septième apéro, alors fais pas chier! Fais ton boulot et remets-moi un jaune, et au trot!
What do you mean I drink too much? It's only my seventh before dinner so don't give me that! Do your job and get me another pastis, and make it snappy!

Le barman, qui était complètement fait, s'était allongé sur le zinc pour roupiller.
The barman, who was completely pissed, had stretched out on the bar to have a kip.

Drinking habits

Je vais toujours au bistrot avec mon clebs pour être sûr de pouvoir retrouver mon chemin.
I always take my dog to the pub with me to be sure of being able to find my way home.

Tous les soirs il allait discuter le bout de gras avec ses potes de bistrot du Café du Commerce et trouvait une solution à tous les problèmes du monde le temps de se jeter cinq ou six canons derrière la cravate.

Every evening he would go and chew the fat with his drinking pals at the Café du Commerce and would set the world to rights in the time it took to knock back five or six glasses of wine.

Il est interdit de séjour au Café des Sports parce qu'il tape le carton pendant des plombes sans rien consommer.

He's barred from the Café des Sports because he plays cards for hours on end without drinking anything.

GLOSSARY

add brandy to one's coffee (to): consoler son café
aperitif: un apéro
bar: le bistrot, le rade, le troquet
barfly: le pilier de bar
Beaujolais: le beaujolpif
beer: la bibine, la mousse, la binouze
bottle: la boutanche; *(of champagne)*: la roteuse; *(of red wine)*: le kil, le litron
brandy: la gnôle; *(bad quality)*: le tord-boyaux
buy a round (to): régaler, rincer
celebrate something with a few drinks (to): arroser quelque chose
cheers!: tchin tchin!, à la tienne/vôtre!
coffee: le petit noir, le jus, le kawa; *(weak)*: le jus de chaussette, le jus de chique
debts: *(in a bar)* une ardoise
down one's drink in one (to): faire cul sec
drink: *(in a bar)* la conso; *to have a drink:* s'en jeter un derrière la cravate, se rincer la dalle, écluser un godet *or* un gorgeon; *to have a drink at the bar:* prendre un verre sur le zinc; *to have one's first drink of the day:* tuer le ver; *drink a lot (to):* picoler, biberonner, lever le coude, téter, avoir la dalle en pente, boire comme un trou; *to drink a whole bottle:* casser la gueule à une bouteille, descendre *or* siffler une bouteille
drop: *(of alcoholic beverage)* une larmichette
drunk: beurré, blindé, bourré, cuit, déchiré, noir, paf, parti, pété, plein (comme une barrique), poivré, rétamé, rond, avoir un coup dans l'aile, avoir son

compte; *to get drunk:* prendre une cuite *or* une bi(t)ture *or* une muflée, se beurrer, se blinder, se bourrer la gueule, se cuiter, se mettre une mine, se noircir, se péter la gueule, se pinter, se poivrer, se rectifier

drunkard: un/une alcoolo, le picoleur, le pochtron, le poivrot, le soûlard

drunkenness: la bit(t)ure, la cuite

empties: les cadavres *(masc.)*

Gauloises® cigarettes: les goldos *(fem.)*

glass: le godet; *(one-litre beer glass):* le sérieux

glass of wine: le canon

head: *(of froth on glass of beer)* le faux-col

hungover (to be): avoir mal aux cheveux, avoir la casquette en plomb *or* en zinc, avoir la gueule en vrac

pastis: le jaune, le pastaga

play cards (to): taper le carton

pub crawling (to go): tirer une bordée

sick as a dog (to be): dégueuler tripes et boyaux

sip (to): siroter

sleep it off (to): cuver

sober up (to): décuiter

stagger (to): avoir du vent dans les voiles, avoir mis les chaussures à bascule

tip: le pourliche

uncork a bottle (to): dépuceler une bouteille

vomit: le dégueulis

vomit (to): dégueuler, gerber

waiter: le loufiat

wine: le pinard; *(red):* le rouquin, le gros qui tache, le brouille-ménage, le picrate

Did you know that

The expressions *prendre une bitture* and
tirer une bordée (see glossary) both derive
from nautical terminology. A *bitture* refers
to a length of cable, and *tirer des bordées*
means "to tack".

Test your rude French

Try and match the sentence in French with its accurate English
translation.

❶ Elle a une sacrée descente; personne n'arrive à la suivre
a) She's a great downhill skier; nobody can touch her
b) She can really knock it back; she can drink everybody under the
table
c) She talks so fast that nobody can understand a word she says

**❷ Il a déménagé à la cloche de bois en laissant des ardoises
dans tous les troquets du quartier**
a) He became homeless, so he had his mail forwarded to various
bars in the neighbourhood
b) He did a moonlight flit and left unpaid bills in all the bars in the
neighbourhood
c) He became seriously deranged and started trading some of the
drawings that he'd done on pieces of slate for drinks in all the
bars of the neighbourhood

**❸ Je l'ai aperçu dans la rue en train de discuter avec un de
ses copains et je peux te dire qu'ils avaient du vent dans les
voiles**
a) I saw him on the street talking to one of his mates and they were
walking so fast they must have been in a hell of a hurry
b) I saw him on the street with one of his mates and they were talking
very volubly to each other
c) I saw him on the street talking to one of his mates and both were
staggering all over the place

RUDE driving

France has a population about the same size as Britain's but it is more than twice as big. This explains why, by British standards, its roads are remarkably uncongested. If you avoid problem areas, you could probably drive thousands of miles in the land of "Bison futé" without encountering a single traffic jam. However, you've got to be ready for every contingency and few skills can be as valuable as that of being able to abuse other drivers (or car mechanics) to dramatic effect. Happy motoring!

A few useful phrases in context

Getting started

J'fais pas 500 bornes dans ton tape-cul, pas question! C'est mauvais pour mes hémorroïdes.
No way am I going 500 kilometres in your old boneshaker! It's bad for my piles.

Au début on s'arrêtait un peu partout, mais à partir du troisième jour on a taillé la route.
To start with we were making quite a few stops, but from the third day on we really ate up the miles.

Saloperie de bagnole de merde! pas moyen de la faire démarrer!
This bastard car refuses to start!

Bragging

Je te dis pas comme je l'ai grillé au démarrage, cette tête de con!
You should have seen how I burnt him up at the lights, the tosser!

On a tapé le deux cents sur le périph à 4 heures du mat'.
We hit 200km an hour on the ring road at 4 in the morning.

Cet enfoiré m'avait fait un bras d'honneur, alors je lui ai fait une de ces queues de poisson!
This dickhead gave me the finger so I cut him right up!

Le poulet sur sa bécane n'arrêtait que les jolies pépées en excès de vitesse; les plus délurées, celles qui savaient y faire, n'avaient même pas à lui montrer leurs papelards pour qu'il les laisse filer sans contredanse...

The motorbike cop only pulled over good-looking birds for speeding; the most brazen ones knew how to get away with it and didn't even have to show him any ID to get let off without a fine.

Rhetorical questions

Où est-ce que tu l'as eu ton permis de conduire? Dans une pochette-surprise?

Where did you get your driving licence? Out of a Christmas cracker?

Et le clignotant, il était en option sur ta caisse pourrie, connard?

Were the indicators an optional extra on that rustbucket of yours, you wanker?

Tu dors, Ducon? Ça fait trois plombes que le feu est passé au vert!

Are you having a nap there, dick-features? The lights have been at green for ages now!

Eh, pauvre type, tu crois vraiment que tu vas pouvoir me doubler avec ton veau?

Do you really think you're going to overtake me in that hairdrier on wheels, you sad git?

Technical problems

Sa caisse bouffe tellement d'essence qu'il s'en sert plus, de peur de tomber en rade entre deux pompes.

His car's so thirsty that he doesn't use it any more in case he runs out of petrol between petrol stations.

La bagnole a drôlement morflé dans les chemins de terre.

The car got totally smashed up on the dirt tracks.

On lui a chouravé les quatre roues de sa caisse et il a ramassé un PV parce qu'il était en zone de stationnement limité...

Someone nicked all four wheels off his car, then he got a ticket cos he was in a restricted parking zone...

Fais gaffe de pas garer ta caisse n'importe où. Y'a des quartiers où les gens se font pas chier à acheter du charbon pour leur barbeuk: ils foutent le feu à une bagnole et puis c'est marre!

Watch where you park your car. In some neighbourhoods people can't be arsed buying charcoal for the barbie, they just set light to a car and off they go!

Drinking and driving

Le routier a sifflé deux bouteilles de rouquin puis il a repris le volant de son 38 tonnes de joyeuse humeur.

The lorry-driver knocked back two bottles of red wine and got back behind the wheel of his 38-tonner in an excellent mood.

On a copieusement arrosé son permis de conduire, puis on est allé faire une virée en bagnole...

We celebrated him passing his test with more than a few drinks, and then took the car out for a spin...

Si je vous souffle dans le poireau, monsieur l'agent, vous me ferez quand même souffler dans le ballon?

If I give you a blow-job, officer, will you still make me blow into the bag?

Accidents

Je me suis fait emplafonner par un abruti qu'était trop occupé à mater le pétard d'une greluche qui passait pour penser à regarder devant lui.

I got smashed into by some idiot who was too busy checking out this bird's arse to remember to look where he was going.

Il a fait fort: il a fusillé sa nouvelle bagnole une semaine après l'avoir achetée!

He's excelled himself this time – he wrecked his car a week after he bought it!

J'ai bigorné ta caisse contre un poteau mais elle est pas trop amochée

I crashed your car into a post but it's not too badly smashed up

Road misery

Quand t'es pris dans un bouchon, qu'il fait 35 degrés, que t'as tes deux mômes qui se battent derrière et ta femme qui te prend la tête, je peux te dire que c'est l'enfer!

When you're stuck in a traffic jam, it's 35 degrees, you've got two kids knocking lumps out of each other behind you and your wife's doing your head in, I can tell you it's hell on wheels!

On est tombé en panne sèche en pleine cambrousse, pas moyen de trouver un garage; les boules!

We ran out of petrol in the middle of nowhere and there wasn't a garage to be found for miles, what a pain!

Avec l'odeur du cigare et les virolos, je sentais que la choucroute que je venais d'avaler ne resterait pas longtemps à sa place.

What with the smell of cigar smoke and the twisty road, I could tell the sauerkraut I'd just eaten was going to make a reappearance before too long.

Il s'est fait aligner par un flic en moto.
A motorcycle cop slapped a fine on him.

Les flics tapaient le carton et discutaient le bout de gras avec les camionneurs qui avaient foutu leurs bahuts en travers de la chaussée pendant que les automobilistes immobilisés, fumasses, cuisaient dans leurs bagnoles en plein cagnard.

The cops were playing cards and chewing the fat with the lorry drivers who had blocked the road with their trucks, while the motorists who they had brought to a standstill were fuming as they sat baking in their cars in the blazing sunshine.

Une petite frappe s'est offert un rodéo au volant de ma Trabant; elle est bonne pour la casse...

This little hoodlum took my Trabant for a joyride and now it's fit for the scrapheap...

On est resté coincé derrière un gros-cul pendant 30 bornes sans pouvoir doubler.

We got stuck behind a juggernaut for 30 kilometres with no way of overtaking.

GLOSSARY

ace driver: un as du volant
bend: *(in the road)* le virolo
boy racer: le jacky
brake (to): donner un coup de patin
break down (to): tomber en carafe *or* en rade
breathalyzed (to be): souffler dans le ballon
breathalyzer: le ballon
cab: le bahut, le tacot
car: la bagnole, la caisse, la charrette, la tire; *(old and in bad repair)*: la guimbarde, la poubelle, le tas de ferraille; *(with poor suspension)*: le tape-cul; *(that lacks power)*: le veau
dent: le pet, le gnon, le chtar
fine: la contredanse, la prune
get lost (to): se paumer
go off the road (to): aller dans le décor, se foutre en l'air
joyriding: le rodéo

kilometre: une borne
lorry: le bahut, le camtar, le gros-cul
motorbike: la bécane, la meule; *(big)*: le gros cube
parking ticket: le papillon
policeman: le bourre, le cogne, le condé, le flic, le poulet
put one's foot down (to): mettre le pied au plancher
rear-view mirror: le rétro
ride: la virée
ring road: le périph'
slow driver: le dort-en-chiant
step on the gas (to): appuyer sur le champignon
Sunday driver: le conducteur du dimanche
traffic warden (female): la pervenche
use a lot of petrol (to): bouffer de l'essence, sucer

Did you know that

French traffic wardens are called *pervenches*
(meaning "periwinkles") because they used
to wear blue uniforms.

Test your rude French

Try and match the French sentence with its accurate English
translation.

❶ Il est allé dans le décor et a encadré un platane
a) He went to an interior decorator's and had a picture representing
    a plane tree framed
b) He went off the road and wrapped his car around a tree
c) He went backstage and smoked a huge joint

❷ Un poulet lui a fait souffler dans le ballon
a) He felt completely bloated after eating a whole chicken
b) The team mascot (a chicken) made him inflate the ball with his
    mouth
c) A cop breathalyzed him

❸ Elle a plié la caisse de son papa
a) She folded a cardboard box for her Dad
b) Her Dad was in stitches listening to her
c) She wrote off her Dad's car

RUDE families

The French writer André Gide famously said "familles, je vous hais" (*I hate you, families*) and the singer Léo Ferré sang "quand je vois un couple, je change de trottoir" (*when I see a couple, I cross the street*): for some, the family is an oppressive and outdated institution that has been responsible for much suffering. For others for whom even divorce is anathema, it is no less than the cornerstone of our civilization.

Whatever your views on the subject, here's a chapter for you and your loved ones.

A few useful phrases in context

Marital bliss

J'en ai marre de toujours me cogner la vaisselle, le ménage et les courses; je suis pas ta bonniche!
I'm sick of always getting lumbered with the dishes, the housework and the shopping; I'm not your slave!

Quelle galère! La belle-doche veut voir les mômes, elle rapplique après-demain et il va falloir se la farcir pendant deux semaines!
What a pain! The mother-in-law wants to see the kids, she's landing on our doorstep the day after tomorrow and we're going to have to suffer her for two weeks!

Il faisait exprès de se taper les encombrements en rentrant du burlingue pour que sa rombière ait moins de temps pour lui prendre la tête une fois rentré au bercail.
He made a point of getting stuck in traffic jams on his way home from the office so that his other half would have less time to get on his back once he got home.

Tous les soirs à sept heures pétantes, tout le voisinage suivait leurs engueulades en direct; les gamins, eux, allaient promener le clébard.

Every evening at seven o'clock sharp, the entire neighbourhood was treated to a live broadcast of their slanging matches; the kids would steer well clear and take the dog for a walk.

Parenting (1)

Son boulot de directrice de crèche est tellement prenant qu'elle a jamais le temps de s'occuper de ses chiards.

Her job as nusery manager takes up so much of her time that there aren't enough hours in the day to look after her own brats.

Leur lardon, il a dix ans mais il a l'âge mental d'un gamin de sept. Vous faites pas de mouron, je leur ai dit, quand il aura 45 berges, il aura l'esprit d'un mec de 42, y'a pas de quoi nous chier une pendule!

Their kid is ten but has a mental age of seven. Don't get stressed out about it, I told them, when he's 45, he'll have the mind of a 42-year-old, so there's no need to make such a song and dance about it!

Elles me font marrer les bourges qui achètent que des produits bio parce que c'est plus écolo et qui conduisent leurs chiards à l'école dans des chars d'assaut qui bouffent du 20 litres aux cent!

These middle-class mums crack me up, buying organic cos they think it's green and then driving their little brats to school in their gas-guzzling Chelsea tractors.

Jusqu'à l'âge de 12 ans le gamin avait idolâtré son vieux; à l'adolescence il lui était subitement apparu comme le dernier des ringards.

Up to the age of 12, the kid had idolized his old man; as soon as he hit puberty he suddenly started seeing him as a sad old square.

Ça s'est passé comme ça: j'étais allé faire la grosse commission derrière un buisson sans savoir que je n'étais qu'à quelques mètres d'un groupe d'ornithologues en planque, qui lorgnaient un specimen rarissime: c'est ainsi que j'ai rencontré celle qui plus tard allait devenir ta maman.

Here's how it happened: I'd gone to have a dump behind a bush, not realizing that I was just a few yards away from a group of ornithologists on stakeout who were looking at an extremely rare specimen: that's how I met the woman who became your mum.

Parenting (2)

Dans ce pays, les bourges, elles ont leurs mômes à l'âge où les prolos elles sont déjà grand-mères.
In this neck of the woods, the posh women have their kids at an age when the chavs are already grandmothers.

> *Je l'ai accompagné au square avec toute sa marmaille.*
> I went to the playground with him and his entire brood.

Leur gamine, celle qu'est ado, elle arrête pas de faire la soupe à la grimace depuis que le paternel lui a interdit d'aller au concert de Franz Ferdinand.
Their teenage girl has been in a huge strop since her old man wouldn't let her go to the Franz Ferdinand concert.

L'autre jour, il y a une mémé de 62 ans qu'a pondu un lardon. Faut espérer que le gamin réclamera pas un frangin ou une frangine!
The other day some old girl of 62 dropped a sprog. Fingers crossed the kid won't start asking for a brother or sister!

Leurs rejetons, ils ont intérêt à se tenir à carreau, sans quoi ils ont vite fait de se prendre une taloche ou un coup de pied au cul.
Their kids have to watch their step, otherwise they get a clip round the ear or a kick up the backside.

Leur vieux était tellement mal vissé qu'il distribuait les beignes à tour de bras, pour un oui, pour un non. Il est tombé en un week-end ce qu'il tombe habituellement en un mois.
Their old man was in such a foul mood that he was dishing out clips round the ear right, left and centre. It rained more blows in one weekend than it normally did in a month.

Breaking up

Cet enfoiré, il a plaqué sa bonne femme parce qu'il trouvait qu'elle commençait à avoir un peu trop d'heures de vol.
The bastard walked out on his wife cos he thought she was starting to look a bit worn round the edges.

"Pourquoi, mais pourquoi est-ce qu'elle m'a largué?", se demandait-il, tout en fouillant dans le panier à linge sale à la recherche d'une paire de fumantes pas trop crades.

"Why, oh why did she dump me?", he wondered, as he rummaged through the laundry basket for a pair of socks that weren't too whiffy.

"Les fayots sont prêts, mais il y a plus une assiette de propre; y'a pas à tortiller il va falloir que je me coltine la vaisselle, puisqu'elle a fait ses valises", se disait-il, avant d'apercevoir le frisbee sur le canapé...

"The beans are ready, but there's no clean plates left. No two ways about it, I'm going to have to tackle the dishes myself now that she's packed her bags", he said to himself, before spotting the frisbee lying on the sofa...

GLOSSARY

brother: le frangin

brother-in-law: le beauf

cat: le minet, le greffier

child: un chiard, un lardon, un gamin (une gamine), un gosse, un loupiot, un merdeux (une merdeuse), un mioche, un môme, un mouflet; *many children*: la marmaille

dog: le cabot, le clébard, le clebs

family (the whole): toute la smala

father: le dab, le daron, le pater, le paternel, le reup, le vieux

husband (my): mon bonhomme, mon Jules, le patron

little madam: une pisseuse

marry (to): se mettre la corde au cou

mother: la maternelle, la reum, la vioque

mother-in-law: la belle-doche; *to be lumbered with one's mother-in-law*: être embellemerdé

old man: un vieux schnoque, un vioque, un pépé

old woman: une vieille bique, une vieille toupie, une vieille peau, une vioque, une mémé

parents: les vieux, les vioques

pregnant (to be): être en cloque, avoir un polichinelle dans le tiroir

shack up with someone (to): se maquer avec quelqu'un

sister: la frangine
son: le fiston, le rejeton
wife (my): ma bourgeoise, ma moitié, la patronne, ma rombière

Did you know that

The words *clebs, smala* (in the glossary above) and many others in French slang (such as *le bled, un chouia, le toubib*) come from Arabic. They entered the French language in the 19th century during the period of French colonial expansion in North Africa.

Test your rude French

Try and match the French sentence with its accurate English translation.

❶ Sa bonne femme est en cloque
a) His wife is pregnant
b) His wife broke out in blisters
c) His wife is a clock-watcher

❷ Son vieux commence à prendre de la bouteille
a) His father has taken to the bottle
b) His father is getting on in years
c) Her husband has been promoted

❸ Je suis bien trop jeune pour me mettre la corde au cou
a) I am much too young to be wearing a tie
b) I am way too young to consider suicide
c) I am much too young to get married

RUDE feelings

If you believe that there is no such thing as black and white but only shades of grey, then perhaps you should skip this section and go straight to the next one. For slang is the ideal medium for expressing one's feelings in no uncertain terms. It definitely isn't the kind of language you can resort to in order to fine-tune a judgement or qualify an opinion.

If you consider that getting your point across is paramount and that offending people is a luxury you can afford, then this section is for you. Actually, as far as slang is concerned, more often than not it's a case of "if you haven't got anything nasty to say, then it's better not to say anything at all".

A few useful phrases in context

It's crap

Déjà son dernier film cassait pas des briques, mais celui-ci, il est carrément nul à chier!
His last film was nothing to write home about, but this one is a pile of shite!

C'est vraiment la zone ce bled, qu'est-ce qu'on peut s'y faire chier!
This place is a complete dump, you really get bored shitless here.

Ils ont fait un tabac avec leur nouveau disque, mais franchement il vaut pas un clou.
Their new record has sold by the bucketload, although frankly it's complete pants.

> *Tirons-nous d'ici, ce troquet est vraiment trop craignos.*
>
> Let's get out of here, this bar is well dodgy.

Annoyance

Elle commence à me plaire cette nana, ça fait trois fois qu'elle me pose un lapin.
That bird's starting to do my head in, that's three times she's stood me up.

Il m'a mis le grappin dessus dès que je suis arrivé et il m'a pas lâché de la soirée; un vrai crampon!
He cornered me as soon as I arrived and stuck to me like glue the whole evening; what a leech!

Tu vas la boucler maintenant? Ça fait trois plombes que tu me pompes l'air avec tes histoires de cul, tu commences à me les casser!
Will you put a bloody sock in it? You've been harping on about your sexploits for three hours now and you're really starting to piss me off.

Ce qu'il peut être enquiquinant leur gamin! Il a fait un boucan pas possible en tapant comme un sourd sur son tambour pendant toute la soirée. Un vrai casse-bonbons!
Their kid can really get on your tits! He made a hell of a racket banging away on his drum like a maniac all bloody night. What a pain in the arse!

Disapproval

Putain, arrête de te la jouer! C'est pas parce que t'es passé à la Caméra Invisible qu'il faut te prendre pour Johnny Depp!
Stop posing about, you arsehole! Just because you've been on Candid Camera doesn't make you Johnny Depp!

Son nouveau petit copain est une espèce de trouduc qui pète plus haut que son cul; il est toujours en train de la ramener.
Her new boyfriend is a complete tosser who thinks his own shit doesn't stink; he's always bloody showing off.

Il est grave mon coloc, plutôt que de changer l'ampoule du salon, il bouquine à la lumière du frigo.
He's not all there, my flatmate. Rather than change the lightbulb in the living room, he uses the fridge light to read his book by.

Appreciation

On s'est vraiment super bien marré à la soirée de Riton, hier soir, c'était vraiment top!
We had an excellent laugh at Riton's party last night, it was top!

Ah ouais! On s'est roulé un joint et on s'est tapé un super délire, c'était trop cool!
Yeah ... we rolled a spliff, it was wicked, man!

Il est crevant le frère de Maurice quand il imite Marcel en train d'imiter Sarkozy; hier il nous a fait une petite séance: la crise!
Maurice's brother is hysterical when he does his impersonation of Marcel imitating Sarkozy; yesterday he put on a show for us and cracked us up!

Il est tellement dingue de sa nana qu'il s'est fait tatouer son portrait dans le dos; comme ça il l'a dans la peau au propre et au figuré!
He's so loved-up with his bird he's had her face tattooed on his back: now he's got her under his skin literally as well as figuratively!

Surprise

Ça m'a soufflé quand elle s'est mise à engueuler son bonhomme comme du poisson pourri devant tout le monde...

I was absolutely flabbergasted when she started bollocking her husband right in front of everybody ...

Qu'il plaque son boulot et sa famille pour entrer dans les ordres, ça m'a laissé sur le cul!

He's quit his job and left his family to become a monk, I can't believe it!

Quoi? Lui, il marche à voile et à vapeur? Alors là, tu m'en bouches un coin!

What, him? He swings both ways? Bloody hell, I'm gobsmacked!

afraid (to be): avoir la frousse *or* la trouille *or* les chocottes *or* les jetons *or* les pétoches, ne pas en mener large, flipper; *(more vulgar)*: faire dans son froc, les avoir à zéro

angry (to be): être en boule, être fumasse, ne pas être jouasse, être en pétard; *to get angry*: se mettre en boule, se mettre en pétard, péter une durite, péter les plombs, péter un câble

annoy somebody (to): bassiner quelqu'un, casser les pieds à quelqu'un, prendre la tête à quelqu'un, courir sur le haricot à quelqu'un; *(more vulgar)*: les brouter à quelqu'un, les casser à quelqu'un, casser les couilles à quelqu'un, faire chier quelqu'un

astound somebody (to): estomaquer quelqu'un, souffler quelqu'un, en boucher un coin à quelqu'un, laisser quelqu'un sur le cul

awful (it is): c'est nul, ça ne vaut pas un clou, ça craint, c'est craignos, c'est de la louse; *(more vulgar)*: c'est merdique, c'est de la merde, c'est (nul) à chier

bad mood (to be in a): être de mauvais poil, être mal vissé, être mal luné, ne pas être à prendre avec des pincettes

bored (to be): s'emmerder, se faire chier

boring: barbant, rasoir, rasant; *(more vulgar)*: chiant (comme la pluie)

chicken out (to): se dégonfler

contemptible individual: un con (une conne),
un connard (une connasse), un enfoiré, un fumier;
(very vulgar): un enculé

coward: un dégonflé

criticize somebody (to): débiner quelqu'un,
pourrir quelqu'un, casser du sucre sur le dos de
quelqu'un

cry (to): chialer

damn (I don't give a): je m'en fiche, je m'en fous,
je m'en balance, j'en ai rien à battre; *(vulgar)*: je
m'en branle, je m'en torche; *(humorous)*: je m'en
tamponne le coquillard

depressed (to be): avoir le bourdon, avoir le cafard

dim (he is): il en tient une couche, il a vraiment pas
inventé l'eau chaude *or* le fil à couper le beurre *or* la
poudre, il est con comme un balai *or* comme la lune,
il est grave

disgust someone (to): débecter quelqu'un, foutre la
gerbe à quelqu'un

distressed (to feel): avoir les boules

edge (to be on): être à cran

go away!: tire-toi!, casse-toi!, dégage!, gicle!

good mood (to be in a): être de bon poil, être bien
vissé, être bien luné

great: génial, super, géant, top, pur, trop bien; *it's
great!*: c'est de la balle!, ça le fait!, c'est de la bombe!,
ça envoie!

grouse (to): râler, rouspéter

hard time (to have a): galérer

have had enough (I): j'en ai ras le bol, j'en ai ma
dose, j'en ai ma claque, j'en ai plein le dos; *(more
vulgar)*: j'en ai ras le cul, j'en ai plein le cul

idiot: une andouille, un con (une conne), un
couillon, un crétin, un gland, une nouille, un trou du
cul, un trouduc, une truffe

irritated (to be): avoir les nerfs, avoir les glandes

laugh (to): se gondoler, se fendre la gueule *or* la
poire *or* la pêche, se marrer

leave someone (to): larguer quelqu'un, plaquer
quelqu'un

leave somebody alone (to): lâcher les baskets à

quelqu'un; *(more vulgar)*: lâcher la grappe à quelqu'un

like it (I): ça me branche, ça me botte, je kiffe ça

love with someone (to be in): en pincer pour quelqu'un, avoir quelqu'un dans la peau, être dingue de quelqu'un

lucky (to be): avoir du bol, avoir du pot; *(more vulgar)*: avoir le cul bordé de nouilles

mediocre (it is): ça casse pas des briques, ça casse pas trois pattes à un canard

messy situation: une galère

mistake (to make a): se gour(r)er, se foutre dedans

mock someone (to): se foutre de la gueule de quelqu'un, charrier quelqu'un

obsessed by something (to be): faire une fixette sur quelque chose

obsession: une fixette

sad (to be): en avoir gros sur la patate, en avoir épais

screwed up (to be): marcher à côté de ses pompes, être barré, être ouf

send somebody packing (to): envoyer balader *or* paître *or* bouler quelqu'un; rembarrer quelqu'un, *(more vulgar)*: envoyer chier quelqu'un

shut up (to): la boucler, la fermer, la mettre en veilleuse; *shut up!*: ta gueule!

speechless (to leave somebody): couper le sifflet à quelqu'un, la couper à quelqu'un

stand him (I can't): je peux pas le voir (en peinture), je peux pas l'encadrer *or* l'encaisser, il me sort par les trous de nez, je peux pas le sentir *or* le blairer *or* le piffer

sulk (to): faire la soupe à la grimace

tacky: ringard, tarte

unpleasant woman: un chameau, une chipie, une garce, une vache

wimp: une lavette, une carpette, une femmelette

worry (to): se faire du mouron *or* du mauvais sang *or* des cheveux

Did you know that

The slang terms *galère* (a messy situation) and *galérer* (to have a hard time) come from Molière's play *Les Fourberies de Scapin* (1671). In a scene where a valet is trying to get some money out of a man by telling him that his son is a galley-slave on a Turkish galley, and can only be freed on payment of a ransom, the father repeats several times "Que diable allait-il faire dans cette galère?" ("what the devil was he doing on the galley?").

Test your rude French

Try and match the French sentence with its accurate English translation.

❶ Il a chopé la grosse tête et il a les chevilles qui enflent
a) He's terribly full of himself
b) His head and his ankles have been swelling
c) He's really annoyed because he was served a beer with a head

❷ Sa femme est un vrai chameau
a) His wife has a very bad stoop
b) His wife is a right bitch
c) His wife is as strong as a horse and is very resilient

❸ Elle s'est laissé embarquer dans une galère par un mec qui craint vraiment
a) She agreed to go on a cruise with a guy who's afraid of sailing on his own
b) She's working for a guy who treats her like a galley-slave
c) She's got into a messy situation with a creepy guy

food

France is deservedly renowned for its superb cuisine. During your stay in the country that boasts more than 300 different types of cheese, why not sample some typical French fare? In order to command the respect of "le garçon", you'll need to commit a few essential terms and phrases to memory. Bon appétit!

A few useful phrases in context

Suggesting an outing to the restaurant

Si on allait bouffer au resto?
Si on se faisait un petit resto?
How about going to a restaurant?

Si on allait bouffer un truc quelque part?
How about going somewhere for a bite to eat?

Commenting on the meal

C'était super chiadé comme bouffe.
It was an ace meal.

La bouffe or *graille était à gerber.*
The nosh was gross.

C'était pas mal mais ça cassait pas des briques or *trois pattes à un canard.*
It wasn't bad but it was nothing to write home about either.

Leur gros qui tache m'a filé une chiasse pas possible.
Their plonk gave me a bad case of the trots.

C'était un boui-boui cradingue, le service était merdique et la bouffe dégueulasse.
It was an awful greasy spoon; the service was shit and so was the food.

Un sauciflard, du brignolet, de la moutarde et un kil de gros rouge, et j'suis un homme heureux.
Some sausage, a bit of bread, mustard and a bottle of red wine and I'm a happy man.

Quand le serveur du resto amerloque lui eut fait comprendre ce qu'étaient les "prairie oysters", elle courut aux chiottes dégueuler tripes et boyaux.
When the waiter in the American restaurant explained to her what prairie oysters were, she ran to the bog and puked her guts up.

Was it plentiful enough?

J'ai les dents du fond qui baignent.
I've really stuffed myself.

On s'en est vraiment foutu plein la lampe.
We really pigged out.

Il y avait à peine de quoi se remplir une dent creuse.
There wasn't enough food to feed a mouse.

Was the service friendly?

Le service? Aux petits oignons, qu'il était!
The service was absolutely great!

Il était aimable comme une porte de prison, le loufiat!
The waiter was an unfriendly sod!

La serveuse était fumasse parce que je lui avais mis la main au panier, et elle a renversé une tasse de kawa sur ma liquette toute propre pour se venger.
The waitress was fuming because I'd goosed her, so she spilled a cup of coffee on my clean shirt to get even.

Was it good value?

C'était génial comme boustifaille et question prix, rien à redire!
The grub was great and the price was right!

On s'est vraiment fait écorcher.
C'était le coup de fusil.
We were fleeced.

Putain, quelle arnaque!
It was a bloody rip-off!

33

aperitif: un apéro
beans: les fayots *(masc.)*, les musiciens *(masc.)*
beer: la mousse, la bibine
bill: la douloureuse
bottle: la boutanche
bread: le bricheton, le brignolet
cheese: le frometon, le clacos; *Camembert cheese*: le calendos, le coulant
coffee: le kawa, le jus, le petit noir; *weak coffee*: le jus de chaussette
cook: le cuistot
eat (to): becter, bouffer, grailler; *(heartily)*: se taper la cloche
empties: les cadavres *(masc.)*
food: la bectance, la bouffe, la boustifaille, la graille
full (to be): caler
hungry (to be): avoir la dalle, avoir les crocs, avoir la dent, claquer du bec, la sauter
insipid: fadasse
meat: la barbaque, la bidoche
potato: la patate
restaurant: le resto, le restau; *(down-market)*: le boui-boui

sandwich: le casse-dalle
starving (to be): crever la dalle
vomit (to): gerber, dégueuler, dégobiller
waiter: le loufiat
water: la flotte, le Château-Lapompe
wine: le pinard; *(red)*: le picrate, le rouquin, le gros qui tache

Did you know that

In French slang beans are called *musiciens* because they tend to cause flatulence and make one break wind due to their starchy content.

Test your rude French

Try and match the French sentence with its accurate English translation.

❶ La bouffe était aux petits oignons; c'est la douloureuse que j'ai eu du mal à digérer
a) There were a lot of onions in the dish I was served and as a result I had a sore stomach
b) The food was great but the price was extortionate
c) We had to walk miles to the restaurant; my feet were hurting so much that it ruined my evening

❷ Leur gros qui tache casse pas trois pattes à un canard
a) The chef doesn't know how to prepare roast duck
b) The waiter spills everything he touches and is unbelievably slow
c) Their house red is nothing to write home about

❸ J'avais pris des musiciens au resto, et je peux te dire que ça a pétaradé pendant toute la nuit!
a) The beans I ate at the restaurant made me fart all night
b) I hired a group of musicians to serenade us during our late-night meal
c) I got into a scrap with a group of buskers outside the restaurant that lasted well into the night

RUDE
foreigners

Although probably not as wary of bloody foreigners as the British and without the benefit of a tabloid press practised in the art of fanning the flames of xenophobia at the slightest opportunity, the French have nonetheless a few choice words to describe the people who have the misfortune of not being like them. Since nothing gives anyone more of a sense of belonging than mocking and excluding others, it could be a good idea to familiarize yourself with the terms most commonly used to stigmatize the non-French. "Vive la différence!" or "l'enfer, c'est les autres"? It's your call!

A few useful phrases in context
Love thy neighbour

Les espingouins ils sont vachement fiers, ils aiment pas ça quand on se fout de leur gueule, mais bizarrement ils sont toujours en train de débiner les portos.
The Dagos are a very proud race; they don't like it when they get the piss taken out of them, yet strangely enough they're always slagging off the Portuguese.

Lui qui peut blairer ni les nègres ni les bougnoules, ça l'empêchait pas de gueuler "allez les Bleus! On va la gagner, la Coupe du Monde! Rentrez-leur dedans à ces sales Ritals!" en regardant sa téloche, ce gros con de franchouillard!
He can't stick Blacks or Arabs but that didn't stop him sitting in front of the telly screaming "Come on the Blues! We're gonna win the World Cup! Sock it to those filthy Eyeties!". Stupid great Frog! [Note: the French team contained many players of foreign extraction.]

L'autre jour un amerloque m'a demandé si la prison de la Bastille pouvait se visiter. J'ai jeté un œil à ma tocante: "c'est pas de bol, vous arrivez trop tard!", que je lui ai fait pour rigoler!
The other day this Yank asked me if you could visit the Bastille prison. I looked at my watch and said "You're out of luck, you're too late!" What a laugh!

Du fait qu'ils ont été occupés par les rebeus pendant des siècles, les espingos ils ont souvent la trouille qu'on les prenne pour des métèques.

Because Spain was occupied by the Arabs for centuries, the Dagos are often worried that people think they're wogs.

Les boches, ils aiment tellement la France qu'ils l'ont envahie trois fois en moins d'un siècle, les salauds!

The Krauts love France so much that they've invaded it three times in less than a hundred years, the bastards!

Multiculturalism

Sa bonne femme fait la classe à un tas de petits niacoués et de petits crouilles, ça doit lui prendre une demi-heure pour faire l'appel: ils ont tous des noms à coucher dehors.

His wife teaches a bunch of little Chinks and towelheads; it must take her half an hour to take the register – their names are all complete tongue-twisters.

Tu verras, dans cette partie de l'Espagne, on parle deux langues: le boche et l'angliche.

You'll see that in this part of Spain they speak two languages: Kraut and Brit.

Il est rital du côté de sa mère et vaguement polack et youpin du côté d'un copain de son père, mais ça l'empêche pas d'être un bon Français.

He's a wop on his mother's side and some sort of Polish yid on the side of his dad's pal, but that doesn't stop him from being a good Frenchman.

All quiet on the Eastern front

Ça leur a tellement bien réussi le passage à l'économie de marché aux russkofs, qu'il y a plein de bonnes femmes qui en sont réduites à aller faire les putes chez les chleubs et les bicots des émirats.

> *Le popov était saoûl comme un polack.*
>
> The Russki was as pissed as a newt.

The Russkis' switch to a market economy was such a great success that many of their women have left to be whores in Krautland and for those towelheads in the Emirates.

Our friends from the countryside

[Note: for many Parisians, country dwellers might as well live in another country.]

Il préférerait crécher à la Santé à Paname, qu'en pleine cambrousse, chez les bouseux.
He'd rather live in the Santé prison in Paris than in the middle of nowhere surrounded by a load of yokels.

Il y a plus d'un péquenaud qui s'est fait des couilles en or grâce au marché noir pendant la guerre.
Many a country bumpkin made a killing during the war thanks to the black market.

Cette fois-ci c'est des patates qu'ils ont déversées devant la préfecture, les culs terreux.
This time it was potatoes the yokels dumped in front of the préfecture.

Dans cette région, c'est tous des ploucs réacs et des culs bénis.
In this part of the country there's nothing but rednecks and Bible-bashers.

GLOSSARY

American: amerloque, ricain, yankee
Arab: arbi, bicot, bougnoule, crouillat, crouille, melon, rebeu *(not particularly offensive)*, raton
black person: bamboula, bronzé, moricaud, nègre
British: angliche, rosbif
Chinese: bridé, chinetoque, jaune, niac, niacoué
country dweller: bouseux, cul terreux, pécore, pedzouille, péquenaud, plouc
devout person: cul béni
French: franchouillard
French of Arab descent: *(male)*: beur; *(female)*: beurette
German: boche, chleuh, fridolin, frisé, fritz
Gypsy: romano, manouche
Italian: macaroni, rital
Jewish: feuj *(not particularly offensive)*, youpin
Polish: polack
Portuguese: portos, tos
Russian: popov, russkof
Spanish: espingo, espingouin

Did you know that

The word *plouc* (meaning "country bumpkin") comes from the name of many Breton villages and towns starting with the sound "Plou-" (as in "Plougastel" or "Ploumanac'h"). Over a long period of time many people from Brittany emigrated to Paris where they were considered uncouth and ignorant by Parisians.

Test your rude French

Try and match the sentence in French with its accurate English translation.

❶ Il aime bien les melons mais il peut pas encadrer les portos
a) He likes melon but he isn't at all fond of port
b) He likes bowler hats better than headwear from Oporto
c) He likes Arabs but can't stand Portuguese people

❷ Je connais une beurette qu'en a tellement marre de la France qu'elle a décidé de mettre les voiles
a) I know a girl from Normandy who decided to sail along the French coastline for a laugh
b) I know a French Arab girl who is so sick of France that she's decided to leave the country
c) I know a French Arab girl who is so sick of France that she's decided to start wearing a veil

❸ Sa bonne femme raffole des macaronis
a) His wife absolutely loves macaroni
b) His wife has a thing for Italian men
c) His wife is raving mad

RUDE health

"Quand la santé va, tout va", as they say in French. This is why France spends colossal amounts of money on a health service which, if a recent survey is to be believed, is the best in the world. This also explains why, in addition to attracting regular tourists, France is now a magnet for health tourists from Britain and elsewhere. Anyway, should you feel a little out of sorts during your stay in the land of the suppository, you'll no doubt want to consult a physician in order to get fit as quickly as possible. An accurate description of your symptoms is central to a sound diagnosis. You've got to be able to help your doctor to help you. That's when this section will come in handy.

A few useful phrases in context

First symptoms

J'arrête pas de graillonner, j'ai mal au crâne: je crois que j'ai attrapé la crève.
I can't stop hawking up phlegm and my head's killing me; I think I've caught my death.

Je pisse des lames de rasoir, docteur. J'ai dû choper quelque chose.
I feel like I'm pissing razor blades, doctor. I think I've caught a dose of something.

Je me sens un peu barbouillé; c'est curieux parce que j'ai pas éclusé plus d'une quinzaine de bières...
I feel a bit queasy. I can't understand it, I only had fifteen beers or so...

Il a la chiasse, et il a gerbé toute la nuit. Les moules devaient pas être fraîches.
He's got the runs and he's been puking all night. The mussels can't have been fresh.

Emergencies

Docteur, venez vite, mon mari s'est pété la gueule en enfilant mes bas! Je crois qu'il s'est cassé une patte.
Doctor, come quickly, my husband fell flat on his face when he was trying on my tights! I think he's broken a leg.

J'ai la couenne complètement cramée par le soleil, j'ai la bloblote et une fièvre de cheval. Quatre plombes à poil en plein cagnard le premier jour, c'était peut-être trop...
My skin's burnt to a crisp and I've got the shakes and a raging fever. Spending four hours starkers in the blazing sunshine on the first day was maybe overdoing it a bit...

Elle s'est charcuté la main en coupant un morceau de barbaque un peu trop duraille.
She cut her hand to ribbons trying to cut a slice of meat that was a bit on the dry side.

At the surgery

Le docteur est tombé dans les pommes quand j'ai enlevé mes fumantes, tellement que ça coinçait.
The doctor keeled over when I took my socks off, the stink was so bad.

J'ai poireauté trois plombes dans un courant d'air pour voir le toubib pour une histoire d'ongle incarné, et j'ai chopé une pneumonie.

I hung about for three hours in a draught waiting to see the doctor about an ingrowing toenail and ended up catching pneumonia.

Elle a tourné de l'œil quand le toubib lui a dit qu'il allait lui faire une piquouse.

She keeled over when the doctor told her he was going to give her a jab.

L'enfoiré, il m'a fait une piqûre pour atténuer la douleur, je l'ai sentie passer!

The bastard gave me a jab supposedly to ease the pain, but boy did I know all about it!

Encore vous! On peut dire que vous avez toujours un pet de travers! Vous avez rien d'autre à foutre que de venir me faire chier dans mon cabinet, si j'ose dire?

You again! There's always something the matter with you! If you don't mind my asking, have you nothing else to do with your time but come to my surgery and piss me off?

Il faut vraiment que je vire mon soutif, docteur? Parce que, vous comprenez, c'est les arpions qui me font souffrir...

Do I really have to take my bra off, doctor? It's my feet that are giving me gyp, you know...

---

anus: un oignon, un trou de balle, un troufignon

behind: le cul, le joufflu, le pétard

breasts: les nénés *(masc.)*, les nibards *(masc.)*, les nichons *(masc.)*, les lolos *(masc.)*, les roberts *(masc.)*

buttocks: les miches *(fem.)*

defecate (to): chier, couler un bronze, faire la grosse commission

dentist: un menteur, un arracheur de dents

diarrhoea: la chiasse, la courante, la foirade; *(as happens to tourists in hot countries)*: la turista

die (to): avaler son bulletin de naissance, calancher, casser sa pipe, clamser, claquer, lâcher la rampe, passer l'arme à gauche

doctor: le toubib

ears: les esgourdes

eyes: les calots *(masc.)*, les châsses *(masc.)*, les mirettes *(fem.)*

face: la poire, la trombine, la tronche, la face

foot: un arpion, un panard, un pinglot

gonorrhoea: la chaude-pisse, la chtouille

hair: les tifs *(masc.)*

hand: la paluche, la pogne

head: la caboche, la cafetière, le ciboulot

heart: le battant, le palpitant

hospital: un hosto

injection: la piquouse

insane (to be): être à la masse, dérailler, travailler du chapeau, déjanter, déménager, avoir un grain, être barjo(t) *or* barge *or* cinglé *or* dingue *or* marteau, avoir une case de vide, être barré, être ouf

leg: la canne, la guibolle, la patte

lungs: les éponges *(fem.)*

mouth: la gueule, le goulot

naked: à poil, à loilpé

nose: le blair, le pif, le tarin

operation (to have an): passer sur le billard, se faire charcuter

penis: la bite, le braquemart, la pine, la queue, le zob

skin: la couenne

sleep (to): en écraser, pioncer, roupiller

spit (to): glavioter

spit (a gob of): un glaviot

testicles: les burettes *(fem.)*, les burnes *(fem.)*, les couilles *(fem.)*, les joyeuses *(fem.)*, les roustons *(masc.)*

tired: flagada, ramollo, raplapla

tooth: le croc, la ratiche

urinate (to): faire la petite commission, pisser

vomit (to): dégobiller, dégueuler, gerber

vulva: la chagatte, la chatte, la cramouille, la foufoune, la minette, le minou, la moule

Did you know that

The expression *passer l'arme à gauche*,
meaning "to die", comes from military
terminology, referring to the position in
which soldiers hold their weapons when they
stand at ease; this is because in French the
expression for "to stand at ease" is "être au
repos", which can also mean "to be resting"
in a non-military context.

Test your rude French

Try and match the French sentence with its accurate English
translation.

**❶ Elle est hyper canon mais tous les mecs la fuient tellement
elle refoule du goulot**

a) She's drop-dead gorgeous but she can't get a man because she's
got chronic halitosis

b) She's very charming but her bad language is enough to drive any
potential boyfriend away

c) She's into firearms but since she's also fond of the bottle, men
keep their distance

❷ Il est passé sur le billard plusieurs fois à cause de son battant

a) He took part in several snooker championships but was always
beaten

b) He had several heart operations

c) He's such a workaholic that he gave up snooker on several
occasions in order to devote more time to his career

**❸ Il avait pas les yeux en face des trous, et j'ai l'impression
qu'il avait salement mal aux cheveux**

a) He had a really bad squint and, in my opinion at least, an absolutely
terrible haircut

b) He had two black eyes and looked as though he'd received some
severe blows on his head

c) He was still half asleep and looked badly hungover

leisure

France offers a vast range of recreational activities that are guaranteed to satisfy even the most demanding of holidaymakers. Scuba-diving, pot-holing, year-round skiing in breathtaking scenery, paragliding, golfing, pétanque, wine-tasting, pot-making, you name it, they've got it. What's more, thanks to a fully integrated transport system, you can reach virtually any destination in trains that are clean, safe, fast, comfortable, affordable and on time, so prepare for a culture shock!

A few useful phrases in context

Transport

Ça a pas été de la tarte pour aller jusqu'à la Gare de Lyon avec tout le populo qu'il y avait en ville. A un poil près, on loupait le train.
It was no picnic getting to the Gare du Lyon as the town was absolutely heaving. We only just managed to catch the train.

Si tu continues à lambiner, on va être à la bourre, le train va nous passer sous le nez, et il faudra poireauter deux plombes avant le prochain! Allez, grouille-toi!
If you keep dawdling, we'll be late, the train will leave without us and we'll have to hang around for two hours waiting for the next one! Come on, get a move on!

Cet abruti de chauffeur de car s'est gourré de route, et on s'est retrouvé sur un champ de manœuvres en plein exercice.
The idiot of a bus driver took the wrong road and we ended up in a military training area right in the middle of some manoeuvres.

Sport

Ce crétin est allé faire du saut à l'élastique en solitaire: il est resté suspendu la tête en bas comme un con pendant trois plombes avant que l'idiot du patelin d'à-côté ne vienne filer un coup de surin dans l'élastique en croyant lui donner un fier coup de main.

The twit went bungee-jumping on his own: he ended up dangling upside down like a complete prick for three hours before the local village idiot came along and cut through the elastic, thinking he was being really helpful.

Ses co-équipiers trouvent qu'il joue tellement perso qu'ils se sont cotisés pour lui acheter un ballon pour lui tout seul.

His team-mates think he hogs the ball so much that they've clubbed together to buy him one of his very own.

Pas question que j'aille dans les buts si ce mec joue en face! Quand il te balance un boulet, rien qu'avec le vent tu t'enrhumes!

No way am I standing in goal if that guy's playing for the other team! When he kicks a ball your way, you'd get a cold just from the rush of air going past your face!

Aux chiottes l'arbitre! C'est pas des binocles qu'il lui faut, c'est une canne blanche et un clébard!
The ref's a total wanker! The guy doesn't need glasses, more like a white stick and a guide dog!

Si je m'inscris à la spéléo ou à l'escalade? Eh bien finalement, je crois que je vais larver devant la télé...
Am I going to sign up for pot-holing or rock-climbing? Well, actually, I think I'm going to veg out in front of the telly...

Le frimeur en combinaison fluo qui dévalait la pente à toute blinde tourna la tête pour mater une petite nénette et se mangea un sapin en pleine gueule.
The poser in his day-glo ski suit who was hurtling down the slope at full speed turned his head to check out some bird and went head-first into a fir tree.

On the beach

Comme il avait paumé sa crème solaire et qu'il avait envie ni de se retaper toute la plage jusqu'aux boutiques, ni qu'on lui pique son emplacement, il décida de se tartiner la couenne avec l'huile des sardines de son pique-nique.
Since he'd lost his sun cream and didn't want to go all the way back along the beach to the shops or, for that matter, lose his place, he decided to smear all over his body the oil from the can of sardines from his picnic.

Tu commences à me les briser menues! Que veux-tu que je fasse à part reluquer les gonzesses? C'est vrai quoi, ça finit par être gonflant d'être là à glander, à regarder le sable et la flotte!
You are really starting to do my head in! What else can I do but check out the birds? It's a drag you know, just lying around with nothing to look at but the sand and the sea!

Toute cette bidoche en train de rôtir sur la plage, franchement ça me débecte. Ça donne envie de devenir végétarien.
The sight of all this flesh roasting on the beach turns my stomach, to tell you the truth. It's enough to make you want to become a vegetarian.

Weather talk

Le petit malin s'était bien gardé de sortir son pébroque de son baise-en-ville quand il s'était mis à vaser; il attendait de pouvoir lorgner les roberts de la nana qui l'accompagnait, une fois qu'elle aurait bien pris la sauce et que son T-shirt serait trempé.

The crafty little devil was careful not to take his umbrella out of his overnight bag when it started bucketing down; he waited so that he could get a good eyeful of the chest on the bird who was with him, after she'd got drenched and her T-shirt was soaking wet.

Merde, faut pas charrier: à la météo ils avaient prévu un soleil à tout casser, moyennant quoi il a plu comme vache qui pisse pendant toute la journée!

This is really taking the piss, the weather forecast said it would be an absolute scorcher, but instead it's been bucketing down all day!

Il est poilant mon pote: "Je suis pas très chaud pour aller au Sahara, et l'Alaska, franchement, ça me laisse froid", qu'il a dit au type de l'agence de voyages!

My mate cracks me up. He said to the travel agent, "The Sahara doesn't sound too hot an idea, and, to tell you the truth, Alaska leaves me cold!"

Memories to cherish

La lune brillait sur le camping; on entendait les ronflements des mecs qui pionçaient, les râles et les jappements des couples qui s'envoyaient en l'air, et les excuses bredouillées des employés que leurs chefaillons continuaient d'emmerder dans leurs songes.

The moon was shining down on the campsite; you could hear the snores of guys who were crashed out, the moans and squeals of shagging couples and the mumbled excuses of the employees whose bosses were still hassling them, even in their dreams.

"Chouette!", se disait-il, "je vais pouvoir emballer les nanas à la teuf de ce soir en dansant la samba!" Finalement, comme ce soir-là les moules de la paella étaient pas fraîches, il a fait tintin pour la samba et il s'est retrouvé à danser la turista entre son pieu et les chiottes pendant toute la nuit.

"Brilliant!" he said to himself. "Dancing the samba at the party tonight is going to be a sure-fire way of pulling the birds!" In the end, however, because the mussels in the paella hadn't been fresh, he forgot about the samba and ended up doing a different kind of dance between his bed and the bog all night.

Le pharmacien, qui s'était jamais aventuré outre-Manche, a cru avoir à faire à un barjot quand le type, un plouc qu'était jamais sorti de son trou, lui tendit plusieurs pelloches à faire développer. "Je suppose que quand vous avez besoin d'aspirines ou de capotes anglaises, vous vous pointez chez le photographe?", qu'il lui a sorti.

The pharmacist, who had never ventured across the Channel, thought he was dealing with a right nutter when the customer, a real yokel who had never been out of his own backyard before, gave him several films to be developed. "I suppose when you need aspirin or durex, you go to the photo shop?" he asked him.

GLOSSARY

TRANSPORT

bicycle: une bécane, un biclo, un clou

boat: *(in bad repair)* un rafiot

car: une bagnole, une caisse, une charrette, une tire; *(old and in bad repair)*: une guimbarde, une poubelle, un tas de ferraille; *(with poor suspension)*: un tape-cul; *(that lacks power)*: un veau

dawdle (to): lambiner

dodge the fare (to): gruger, truander

helicopter: un hélico

hurry (to): se magner (le cul), se grouiller

late (to be): être à la bourre

leave (to): mettre les voiles, mettre les bouts, les mettre, lever l'ancre

miss the train (to): louper le train

motorbike: une bécane, une meule; *(big)*: un gros cube

plane: un zinc; *(old)*: un coucou

rollerblades: les rollers *(masc.)*

train: le dur

underground (the): le tromé, le trom

wait (to): poireauter, faire le poireau

SPORT

body-building: la muscu

football: le foot

goalkeeper (incompetent): la passoire

graze the goal post (to): tutoyer le poteau

hog the ball (to): jouer perso

horse: un bourrin, un canasson

nets (the): la cage

nutmeg: un petit pont; *to nutmeg somebody*: faire un petit pont à quelqu'un

penalty: le péno

powerful kick: un boulet, une patate, une praline

predictable: *(of move, kick, pass)* téléphoné

stall for time (to): jouer la montre

swim (to): faire trempette, se baquer, piquer une tête

thrash someone (to): mettre la pâtée à quelqu'un, mettre la piquette à quelqu'un, dérouiller quelqu'un

thrashing: une branlée, une déculottée, une dérouillée, une dégelée, une tripotée, une tannée, une piquette, une branlée

win hands down (to): *(in a race)* arriver dans un fauteuil

THE WEATHER

apply sun cream (to): *(generously)* se tartiner de crème solaire

bitter cold: un froid de canard; *it's bitterly cold*: il fait un froid de canard

burn (to): cramer

cold (it's): ça caille, on se les gèle, on crève de froid, on se pèle

fog (thick): la purée de pois

get drenched (to): se faire saucer, se faire rincer, prendre la flotte

pouring (it's): il tombe des cordes

rain (to): flotter, vaser

scorching (it's): ça cogne, ça tape, on crève de chaleur

shower (a): une saucée, une rincée

sun: le cagnard

umbrella: un pépin, un pébroque, un riflard

ART

bad movie: un navet

daub (a): une croûte

film (a): *(for cameras)* une pelloche

movies (the): le cinoche, le ciné; *to go to the movies*: aller au cinoche, se faire une toile

music: la zicmu, la zizique

ticket (a): un biffeton

Did you know that

In football slang the expression *mettre la soutane* (*soutane* = "cassock") means "to avoid getting nutmegged" because it would be all but impossible to kick the ball between your opponent's legs if he was wearing a cassock...

Test your rude French

Try and match the French sentence with its accurate English translation.

❶ Ils leur ont mis la pâtée

a) They served them dog food
b) They served them pâté
c) They thrashed them good and proper

❷ On a eu droit à la purée de pois pendant toutes nos vacances en Bretagne

a) We were served mushy peas every single day during our stay in Brittany
b) Throughout our holiday in Brittany, farmers protested by dumping potatoes onto the roads
c) The weather was incredibly foggy throughout our holiday in Brittany

❸ Elle m'a emmené voir un navet qui n'en finissait pas

a) She took me to a place where I was shown an incredibly long turnip
b) She took me to see a film that was both really bad and very long
c) She took me to a doctor who kept us waiting for ages

RUDE nightclubbing

"Clubbing" is one of the favourite leisure pursuits of today's youth all across Europe, and France is no exception. There are even magazines dedicated to this strange pastime which consists mainly in gyrating in the midst of a deafening racket, drinking oneself into a stupor and occasionally popping dangerous pills. Who would subject oneself to such torture if it wasn't in the hope of finding a suitable partner for amorous activities? We've decided to include this chapter even though you're highly unlikely to hear anything people might attempt to tell you once you've passed the door of a nightclub.

A few useful phrases in context

"Talent" spotting

Dans les chiottes, trois morues en train de se ravaler la façade parlaient mecs en gloussant.
In the toilets, three tarts were putting on their warpaint and having a chuckle about the talent.

Hé, mate un peu la nana accoudée au bar; il y a du monde au balcon!
Hey, check out that bird up at the bar, you don't get many of those to the pound!

Vise un peu le mec avec les gros biscoteaux et les petites miches là-bas! Il est vraiment craquant!
Check out the guy with the bulging biceps and the cute buns over there! He's well fit!

Health hazards

Il est devenu sourdingue à force de passer toutes ses soirées en boîte.
He spent so many evenings clubbing that he ended up going deaf.

Ils font tellement gueuler la sono que c'est impossible de faire du gringue aux gonzesses sans attraper une extinction de voix.

They turn the music up so loud in that place that it's impossible to chat up the birds without losing your bloody voice.

À ta place j'essaierais pas de lever la meuf avec les gros roberts; à ce qu'on dit il y a que le train qui lui est pas passé dessus. Tu risquerais de choper une saloperie.

If I were you I wouldn't try to get off with that bird with the big tits; apparently she's slept with everything that moves. You might catch something nasty.

Disappointment

Kevin rageait d'avoir claqué 100 euros en boîte à payer des verres aux gonzesses, pour en fin de compte rentrer la pine sous le bras...

Kevin was fuming because he'd blown over sixty quid in the nightclub buying drinks for girls he was trying to get off with, only to come home without having pulled at all...

Ce crétin a branché une superbe créature qu'il avait repérée au bar mais s'est aperçu un peu tard qu'il fallait pas se fier aux apparences...

The dickhead picked up this gorgeous creature he spotted at the bar only to realize too late that appearances can be deceptive...

Après une demi-douzaine de tentatives pour trouver une nana avec qui danser, et après s'être pris autant de vestes, il décida de changer de crémerie.

After getting the brush-off from the few girls he asked to dance with him, he decided to try his luck somewhere else.

Il avait viré son alliance pour pouvoir draguer les petites minettes plus à l'aise, mais son bronzage le trahissait tout autant que sa bagouse.

He'd taken off his wedding ring so that he could chat up the birds more easily, but his suntan gave the game away just as much as his ring would have.

Violence

Deux mecs se sont frités à la sortie de la boîte parce qu'il y en a un qu'avait mis la main au cul de la copine de l'autre, tu vois le genre...

Two guys got into a scrap outside the club because one of them had tried to feel up the other guy's girlfriend, you can imagine the scene...

Il supporte pas qu'on mate sa meuf, qui pourtant se balade toujours dans une jupe ras la touffe hyper moulante et les nibards aux trois quarts à l'air.

He can't stand other guys eyeing up his girlfriend, though she always goes around in a tight mini-skirt up to her arse and with her tits hanging out.

Calmos les mecs! Vous allez quand même pas vous bigorner pour une pétasse! Y'a de la fesse pour tout le monde ici...

Take it easy guys! You're not going to have a fight over a bird! There's plenty of totty for everyone here!

Sad...

Sur la piste de danse un pauvre type se la jouait pendant que toutes les souris se foutaient de sa gueule. Grave!

Some jerk was strutting his stuff on the dance floor and all the girls were taking the piss out of him. Sad!

Le jeune mec sentait tellement la cocotte que même les nanas les moins farouches décanillaient quand il rappliquait.

The guy reeked so much of aftershave that even the biggest slappers fled as soon as he came near them.

Il croyait faire un effet bœuf avec son nouveau futal fluo et hyper moulant, mais finalement il a réussi qu'à faire un effet beauf.
He thought he'd look like a real man-about-town in his new day-glo, skin-tight trousers, but in the end he only succeeded in looking like an Essex Man.

Sa vague ressemblance avec un chanteur à la mode lui assurait une cote pas possible auprès de la nuée de sauterelles qui s'abattait sur la boîte tous les soirs.
Because he looked a bit like a well-known singer he always got mobbed by the birds who hung out at the club every night.

GLOSSARY

badly dressed (to be): être mal ficelé, être mal fagoté, être fagoté comme l'as de pique
beat up (to): arranger, casser la gueule à, faire une tête au carré à, foutre une raclée à
bored stiff (to be): se faire chier comme un rat mort
bouncer: le videur
chat up (to): draguer, faire du plat à, faire du gringue à, brancher
cigarette: la clope, la tige, la garo(t), la peuclo
classy: classe, classieux
cocaine: la coco, la coke, la neige, la reniflette
crap: merdique, nul; *(stronger)*: à chier
curvaceous: bien bousculée, bien roulée
Don Juan: le tombeur
dress smartly (to): se fringuer *or* se saper très classe
drug addict: le/la toxico
ecstasy: un *or* une ecsta, un *or* une X
erection (to have an): bander, triquer, avoir la trique
eye (to give someone the): faire de l'œil à quelqu'un
eye up (to): mater, reluquer
fight: le baston, la castagne; *(between women)*: le crêpage de chignon
French kiss somebody (to): rouler une pelle *or* un palot *or* un patin à quelqu'un
get off with (to): emballer, lever, tomber

girl: *see* woman

great: super, génial, top, pur

hangups (full of): coincé

haschisch: le shit, le hasch

heroin: la blanche, l'héro *(fem.)*, la poudre, la chnouf

high: *(on drugs)* défoncé, raide, raide-def

impression (to make an): faire un effet bœuf

look great (to): avoir un look d'enfer

marijuana cigarette: le pétard, le tarpé, le splif

miniskirt *(very short)*: la jupe ras-la-touffe

music: la zicmu, la zizique

nightclub: la boîte

party (a): une teuf, une chouille, une bringue; *a party animal*: un teufeur

party (to): faire la bringue, faire la teuf, teufer, faire la chouille, chouiller

rebuffed (to be): se prendre une veste

record (a): un skeud

score (to): faire une touche, emballer

see you later!: à plus!, à tout'!

sex (to have): baiser, tirer un coup, se mélanger; *(of man)*: baiser, ramoner, tirer, tringler

sound system: la sono

tease (a): une allumeuse

trendiness: la branchitude

trendy: tendance, branché; *(pejorative)* branchouille

vulgar: vulgos

wild time (to have a): s'éclater

woman, girl: la gonzesse, la meuf, la nana, la pépée, la sauterelle; *(beautiful)*: la bombe, le canon; *(ugly)*: le boudin, le cageot, le thon; *(with small breasts)*: la planche à pain *or* à repasser; *(vulgar or easy woman)*: la grognasse, la greluche, la morue, la pétasse; *(overly made-up)*: le pot de peinture

Did you know that

The expression *être mal fagoté,* meaning "to be badly dressed", comes from the word *fagot,* "a bundle of wood". The image is that of a bundle of wood badly tied together.

The word *chnouf*, meaning "heroin", comes from the German "Schnupftabak", a word that means "snuff".

Test your rude French

Try and match the French sentence with its accurate English translation.

❶ **On est allé dans une boîte où il y avait trois pelés et un tondu**
a) We went to a nightclub patronized by skinheads
b) We went to a nightclub that was almost completely deserted
c) We went to a nightclub where the talent was scarce

❷ **Il lui a proposé la botte après seulement un slow**
a) He asked her to sleep with him after just one slow dance
b) He tried to sell her drugs after they had a slow dance
c) He tried to flog her a pair a boots after they had a slow dance

❸ **Dès que je l'ai vue elle m'a tapé dans l'œil**
a) The first time I saw her she hit me in the eye
b) I took an immediate fancy to her
c) The first time I saw her I thought she was immensely irritating

RUDE
policing

Whether you travel to France with your family looking for sunshine and good food or with your mates looking for aggro at football matches, you might very well have to deal with the police at some point during your stay there. Should you belong to the latter group, it would be wise to brush up on your crime-related slang if you want to be able to hold a conversation with your cellmates while awaiting deportation back to Blighty. And one piece of advice: English humour doesn't always travel well, so don't try your Inspector Clouseau impersonation on a member of the French police force.

A few useful phrases in context

Identifying a suspect

C'est un maigrichon d'environ cinquante berges qu'a une casquette en peau de fesse et une barbouze.

He's a skinny guy, around fifty, as bald as a coot, with a beard.

C'est une armoire à glace d'environ 35 balais, avec des biscoteaux énormes, un œil qui dit merde à l'autre, et un tutu rose.

He's built like a brick shithouse, around 35, with huge biceps, he's cross-eyed and he's wearing a pink tutu.

C'est une morue, plate comme une limande et avec une gueule de raie qui travaille pour un maquereau du côté du boulevard Poissonière.

She's a hooker, as flat as a pancake and with a real fish face, who works for a pimp somewhere around the boulevard Poissonière.

Ils étaient deux: un gros lard qui se déplumait et une grande perche maigre comme un clou.

There were two blokes: one was a big fat guy going bald and the other was a long streak of piss.

Elles étaient deux: une gonzesse super bien roulée avec des guiboles de rêve, le contraire du boudin, et sa copine, une espèce de pot à tabac.

There were two birds: one was really curvy with great legs, no dog, that's for sure, but her friend was a dumpy shortarse.

Trouble with the law

Hé Bébert! Les mecs qu'on a épinglés pour délit de sale gueule ce matin, il faut les relâcher: ils jouent contre le quinze de France cet aprème.

Oi, Bébert! Those guys we nabbed this morning coz we didn't like the look of them, we need to let them go... they're playing rugby against France this afternoon.

Le keuf, qui s'était mis dans la tête d'apprendre l'anglais, alpaguait des rosbifs et des amerloques pour un oui pour un non et les foutait au gnouf pour pouvoir faire la converse avec eux pendant ses heures de service.

The cop, who had taken it into his head to learn English, would arrest Brits and Yanks at the drop of a hat and throw them into the slammer so that he could practise his conversational skills with them while he was on duty.

Hier, il y a des racailles qu'ont foutu le feu à des poubelles et quand les pompiers sont arrivés ils se sont fait caillasser!

A bunch of yobs set fire to some bins yesterday, and when the fire brigade turned up they got pelted with stones!

Quand le guetteur a gueulé "22!", on s'est tous débinés dare-dare.

When the guy on lookout shouted "watch it!" we all legged it.

Au moment de passer les bracelets au suspect, le flic se souvint soudain qu'elles étaient toujours attachées au plumard et à sa bonne femme...

As he was about to put the cuffs on the suspect, the cop suddenly remembered that they were still attached to the bed ... and to his wife.

Il a écopé de cinq ans à l'ombre.

He copped a five-year stretch.

Aggro

Les deux poulets passèrent le touriste à tabac histoire de se réveiller un peu après leur petit roupillon, puis ils écoutèrent d'une oreille distraite son histoire de bagnole qu'on lui avait chouravée avec toute son oseille et sa valoche dedans....

The two cops gave the tourist a hammering just to wake themselves up a bit after their nap, then they half-heartedly listened to his story of his car that had got nicked with all his cash and his suitcase inside it.

Je vous préviens les mecs, faites gaffe quand vous l'interrogerez, c'est un coriace: je me suis fait super mal à la pogne en lui cognant dessus...

I'm warning you, guys, watch out when you question him, he's a tough one: I really hurt my hand when I punched him.

Ah! Ah! Mort de rire! Lui qu'est toujours en train de râler parce qu'on vit dans une société hyper fliquée, il était pas jouasse quand il s'est fait taxer son blouson, son fute et ses godasses par deux malabars. "Mais que fait la police?", qu'il demande maintenant.

Ha ha ha! Hilarious or what? He's always whinging that we live in a police state, but he wasn't too happy when two big bruisers nicked his jacket, his keks and his shoes. "What the hell are the police doing about it?" he's asking now.

Il a fait mine de lui filer une pêche dans la poire, et l'autre est tombé dans les pommes.

He made as if to land him one in the face and the other guy keeled over.

GLOSSARY

CRIME AND VIOLENCE

arrest (to): agrafer, alpaguer, cueillir, embarquer, épingler, gauler

bank robber: un braqueur

bank robbery: un braquage de banque, un casse

beat up (to): arranger, casser la gueule à, cogner, faire une tête au carré à, foutre une raclée à, passer à tabac

black eye: un coquard, un œil au beurre noir

blow: une beigne, une châtaigne, un marron, une pêche, un pain

bullet: une bastos, un pruneau, une valda

confess (to): se mettre à table, manger le morceau,

casser le morceau, s'allonger

demonstration: une manif

denounce (to): balancer

escape (to): se faire la belle, se faire la paire

fight: le baston, la castagne

flee (to): se barrer, se débiner, mettre les bouts, calter, se casser, foutre le camp, se tailler, trisser, prendre ses jambes à son cou

gun: le flingue, le pétard, le calibre

handcuffs: les bracelets *(masc.)*

hideout: la planque

hold-up: un braquage

hold up a bank (to): braquer une banque

identification papers: les fafiots *(masc.)*, les papelards *(masc.)*

informer: un indic

kill (to): buter, descendre, faire la peau à, zigouiller

knife: le surin, le schlass

lie (a): un craque, un bobard

life sentence (to get a): être condamné à perpète

loose (to be on the): être en cavale

motorcycle policeman: une vache à roulettes

police (the): les flics *(masc.)*, les poulets *(masc.)*, la poulaille, les condés *(masc.)*, les cognes *(masc.)*; *to have the police on one's tail*: avoir la police au cul

police van: le panier à salade

policeman: un bourre, un bourrin, une bourrique, un cogne, un condé, un flic, un poulet, un perdreau, une vache; *(more modern)*: un keuf, un schmitt; *a corrupt policeman*: un ripou

prison (in): en cabane, au frais, à l'ombre, au placard, en taule

prison cell: le gnouf

send someone to prison (to): mettre quelqu'un au frais *or* à l'ombre, coffrer quelqu'un

stab (to): suriner

stakeout (to be on a): être en planque

steal (to): barboter, chiper, chouraver, faucher, gauler, piquer, tirer

stone (to): caillasser

stoning: le caillassage

yob: une racaille, une caillera, une caille, un lascar

DESCRIPTIONS (*see also glossary in the Rude Nightclubbing section*)

bald (to be): ne plus avoir un cheveu sur le caillou, avoir une casquette en peau de fesse

big strong man: une armoire à glace, un balaise, un malabar

cross-eyed (to be): avoir les yeux qui se croisent les bras, avoir un œil qui dit merde à l'autre

curvaceous: bien bousculée, bien roulée

fat man: un gros lard, un gros plein de soupe

fat woman: une grosse vache

flat-chested (to be): être plate comme une limande *or* comme une planche à pain

man: un mec

old man: un vieux schnoque, un vioque, un pépé

old woman: une vieille bique, une vieille toupie, une vieille taupe, une vioque

shaved head (to have a): avoir la boule à zéro

skinny: maigrichon

tall thin girl: une grande gigue

tall thin person: une asperge, une grande bringue, une grande perche

woman: une gonzesse, une meuf, une nana

Did you know that

The origin of the expressions *se mettre à table* and *manger le morceau*, meaning "to confess" dates back to the time when suspects were deliberately starved by the police in order to force them to confess. They were only given food once they had agreed to confess, hence the expressions.

Test your rude French

Try and match the French sentence with its accurate English translation.

❶ Il a pris trois pruneaux dans le buffet
a) He was shot three times in the chest
b) He took three prunes from the cupboard
c) He hardly ate anything at the buffet

❷ Son vieux est poulet
a) His old man is a real chicken
b) His Dad is a cop
c) His father is a very arrogant man

❸ Il a passé six mois à l'ombre
a) He was in hospital for six months
b) He was suspended for six months
c) He spent six months inside

RUDE
schools

"Tête bien faite vaut mieux que tête bien pleine" (*it's better to know how to use one's head than to have a head full of facts*), goes the saying (even though, if one wants to be pedantic about it, the French philosopher Montaigne used the expression about masters, not students). However, most would agree that "tête bien faite et bien pleine" (*an agile mind and a head that's full of facts*) is even better and parents expect nothing less from the school system. Should you decide on a prolonged stay in the land of Descartes, you'll have the opportunity of sending your children to school for free from a very young age. But as they get older, they'll acquire a whole new vocabulary which this section will help you decipher.

A few useful phrases in context

Different strategies

Le gamin, qui s'était couvert les bras et le bide d'antisèches, avait oublié qu'il avait une séance de pistoche avant l'interro de maths.
The kid had written the answers all over his arms and stomach, forgetting that he had swimming before the maths test.

J'ai les boules: j'étais censé me taper tout "À la recherche du temps perdu" mais j'en ai pas lu une ligne et j'ai une interro dans une heure. Ça cause de quoi, en deux mots?

I'm totally stressed out here: I was meant to read all of "In Search of Lost Time" but I haven't looked at a single line of the thing and now I've got a test in an hour. What's it about, in a couple of words?

Il a potassé toute la nuit, a eu une panne d'oreiller le lendemain matin, s'est pas pointé à l'exam et s'est chopé une bulle.

He swotted like crazy all night, slept in the next morning, never turned up for the exam and got a big fat zero.

What's your favourite subject?

Comme il avait déconné dans le labo pendant le cours de bio, la prof lui a donné des exos à faire pendant la récré.

As he'd been pissing about in the lab during the biology lesson, the teacher gave him exercises to do during the break.

Je suis une brêle en maths, j'entrave que dalle à toutes ces histoires de trigonométrie; il va falloir que je truande sinon je vais me rétamer.

I'm hopeless at maths, I don't understand a bloody thing about this trigonometry lark; I'm going to have to cheat if I don't want to fail the thing.

Pour tchatcher, il en connaît un rayon mais faut pas trop lui demander de se creuser le ciboulot.

He knows a thing or two about chatting but when it comes to actually using his brain that's quite another matter.

La seule matière où tu peux pas pomper, c'est la gym.

The only subject you can't cheat in is PE.

Hard luck

Je croyais me promener en géo, mais finalement je me suis fait étendre; je me suis foutu dedans, j'ai confondu Haïti avec Tahiti, et la Slovaquie avec la Slovénie.

I thought geography was going to be a piece of cake but I ended up failing big time; I confused Haiti with Tahiti and Slovakia with Slovenia.

Ça faisait deux heures qu'il planchait quand le repas pris au RU est remonté sans prévenir, et il a tout gerbé sur sa copie.
It was two hours into the exam when the meal he'd had in the canteen came back up without any warning and he puked the lot up all over his paper.

Education, education, education

Le premier ministre fait une fixette sur l'éducation, mais il les lâche pas facilement question budget, et il arrête pas de taper sur les doigts des profs.
The prime minister has education on the brain but he's a real tightwad when it comes to the budget for it and he's always rapping the teachers over the knuckles.

Leur gamin fait pas vraiment d'étincelles à l'école mais ils se font pas de mouron, ils l'enverront dans une boîte privée.
Their kid isn't exactly the sharpest knife in the drawer but they're not bothered, they're just going to send him to a private school.

Ils ont changé de patelin pour que leur rejeton puisse aller dans un bahut pas trop pourri.
They moved to a different town so that their kid can go to a better school.

GLOSSARY

badly presented paper: un torche-cul
brainwashing: du bourrage de crâne
break: la récré
chat (to): tchatcher
cheat (to): truander
copy (to): pomper (**from someone** sur quelqu'un)
cram (to): bachoter
cramming: le bachotage
crib (a): une antisèche
cut a class (to): sécher un cours
dash off a piece of work (to): torcher un devoir
dictionary: un dico
dunce: un cancre
essay: une disserte, une rédac
exercise (an): un exo
exert oneself (to): se casser la nénette, se casser le tronc
fail (to): se planter, se rétamer, se faire étendre

geography: la géo
good at maths (to be): être matheux
head of the school (the): le dirlo
intelligent person: une tête, une tronche
laze about (to): buller
lucky (to be): avoir du bol *or* du pot
mistake (to make a): se gourrer, se foutre dedans
nought: une bulle
physical education: la gym
private school: une boîte privée
pupil: le potache
rack one's brains (to): se creuser le ciboulot, se creuser les méninges
secondary school: le bahut
stuck (to be): *(during an exam)* sécher
study (to): potasser
take an exam (to): plancher
test: une interro
understand (to): piger, entraver
university: la fac
university canteen: le RU *(short for* "restaurant universitaire")
unlucky (to be): avoir la poisse, ne pas avoir de pot *or* de bol
unruly (to be): déconner, faire le con
wide of the mark: à côté de la plaque, à la ramasse
work hard (to): bûcher

Did you know that

French slang words have a wide range of origins. For instance, the word *truander* ("to cheat") comes from *truand* (meaning "a gangster"), a Gaulish word meaning "a vagabond", related to the Irish *truagh*, meaning "wretched", and the term *tchatcher* comes from the Spanish *chacharear* ("to chat"). Originally, the word *bûcher* (from *bûche*, "a log"), meaning "to work hard" in slang, used to mean "to fell trees".

Test your rude French

Try and match the sentence in French with its accurate English translation.

❶ **Mon frangin, il est vraiment trapu en physique**
a) As far as physique is concerned, my brother is very squat
b) My brother is excellent at physics
c) My brother is useless at physics

❷ **Elle arrête pas de buller en classe**
a) She does sod all at school
b) She always gets very bad marks at school
c) She keeps popping her bubble gum during lessons

❸ **Ils ont trouvé un bon bahut pour leur fils**
a) They found a good secondary school for their son
b) They found a great sideboard for their son
c) They have acquired a lorry for their son

RUDE sex

NB: Readers of a delicate disposition are advised that this section contains material of a crude nature.

According to scientists, the average adult male thinks more often about sex than about all other possible topics combined. (The data concerning females is more difficult to ascertain.) In view of these extraordinary figures, we have decided to devote an extended section to a subject that features so prominently in people's minds. Contrary to popular belief, the French are not the sex-crazed nation that they are often portrayed as, and you're probably as likely to find a sexy young thing ready to hop into bed with you at the drop of a hat as you are to see a Frenchman dressed in a beret and a striped shirt wearing onions around his neck. In any case, sex is without a doubt one of the most generative fields as far as slang is concerned, and this subject alone could fill several volumes.

A few useful phrases in context

Arousal… or not

Jean-Pierre bandait tellement qu'il éprouva quelque difficulté à lever son cul de sa chaise pour aller jusqu'au bar.
Jean-Pierre had such a stonking hard-on that he had some difficulty getting out of his chair to go to the bar.

Anne-Sophie se rendit compte avec satisfaction qu'Édouard triquait comme un malade; la soirée s'annonçait bien.
Anne-Sophie was pleased to note that Édouard had an enormous boner; the evening had got off to a promising start.

Quand Maryse sortit finalement de la salle de bain, Sébastien avait débandé depuis longtemps et ronflait comme un bienheureux.
By the time Maryse eventually emerged from the bathroom, Sébastien had lost his hard-on hours before and was snoring like a pig.

La vue des traces de pneu sur le froc du mec lui coupa net l'envie de faire un gros câlin.

Seeing skidmarks on the guy's keks killed any desire she had of giving him a big cuddle stone dead.

Self-help

Le gros dégueulasse, la pogne dans la fouille de son futal, se branlait en douce en regardant les cuisses de la nana assise en face de lui.

The filthy pig had his hand in his trouser pocket and was having a sly wank as he checked out the thighs of the bird sitting opposite him.

Comme il avait pas réussi à lever de gonzesse, il décida de se rabattre sur la veuve Poignet.

Since he hadn't managed to pull, he decided to resort to having a tug instead.

À force de se polir le chinois, Jules avait chopé des vaches de valoches sous les châsses.

Jules had been wanking so much that he had bags under his eyes that were more like suitcases.

Sex as a commodity

"T'as baisé, maintenant il faut banquer mon coco!", dit la morue au jeune blanc-bec qui croyait avoir fait une touche.

"You've had your fun, now let's see your money!", said the whore to the innocent young guy who thought he'd pulled.

"50 euros! C'est 50 euros la pipe!", hurla la prostituée dans l'oreille du monsieur bien mis qui avait la malchance d'être dur de la feuille.

"50 euros! It's 50 euros for a blow-job!", yelled the prostitute in the ear of the well-dressed man who had the misfortune to be hard of hearing.

Je suis allé voir un film de cul pas piqué des vers l'autre jour, y'avait plus de barbus que dans un meeting de fondamentalistes islamiques.

I went to see a great porn movie the other day, there was more pussy than at a cat breeders' convention.

The love that dares not speak its name

Madame rentra plus tôt que prévu et trouva le majordome en train de besogner Monsieur sur le tapis du salon.
Madame came home earlier than expected and found the butler humping her husband on the living-room carpet.

C'est uniquement lorsqu'un torchon à sensation publia des photos du ministre en train de se faire mettre par un pédé cuir que sa cote de popularité commença à dégringoler.
It was only when a tabloid published photos of the minister getting shafted by a queer in full leather that his popularity rating began to slump.

Surpris par le sergent de semaine en train de s'enfiler joyeusement dans les douches, ils prirent dix jours de gnouf chacun; ordre fut donné de ne pas les mettre dans la même cellule.
Caught unawares by the sergeant on duty that week shagging merrily away in the showers, they each got ten days in the cooler; the order was given not to put them in the same cell.

Mais non, vous foutez pas de ma gueule les mecs, j'suis pas une tarlouze, j'suis bi!
No, no, no, guys, don't take the piss, I'm not a poof, I'm bi!

Lui qui crachait pas sur un petit peep-show lesbien de temps en temps, il a trouvé ça vachement moins bandant quand sa bonne femme s'est barrée avec une gouine.
Although he didn't say no to going to a lesbian peep-show from time to time, he found it a lot less of a turn-on when his wife ran off with a dyke.

Scoring

Elle accepta les avances du nain, ayant entendu dire que malgré leur petite taille, ces êtres étaient souvent montés comme des taureaux.
She let the dwarf come onto her quite happily, having heard that despite their lack of stature, they were often hung like donkeys.

Sous la lumière crue du lampadaire il s'aperçut que la "jeune minette" – qu'il avait draguée dans la pénombre de la boîte de nuit et qu'il ramenait maintenant chez lui – avait en fait pas mal de kilomètres au compteur.

Under the harsh light of the street lamp he saw that the "young thing" he'd chatted up in the dimly lit nightclub and was now taking home had in fact been round the block a few times.

Les gonzesses l'adorent bien qu'il soit pas bien beau et guère plus malin: il paraît qu'il a un engin d'un pied de long...
The women love him even though he's nothing to look at and no better in the brains department; it seems he's got a dick a foot long...

Pas question que je te laisse mes clés pour la soirée! C'est la troisième fois en une semaine! C'est pas un baisodrome mon apart, alors démerde-toi!
No way am I leaving you my keys for the evening! That's the third time in a week! My flat's not a bloody brothel, sort it out yourself!

Sa sœur est une sacrée dragueuse, elle s'attaque même aux vioques de la maison de retraite de sa grand-mère...
His sister's a terrible one for chatting up men; she even launches herself on the old geezers in her granny's nursing home...

Adultery

Ce crétin s'est amouraché d'une espèce de petite greluche alors qu'il a une femme formidable et qui baise vachement bien en plus... Hein? Quoi? J'ai fait une gaffe?...

Sa femme, c'est une vraie voleuse de santé: je suis sur les rotules!
His wife is a real goer; I'm absolutely shagged!

The fool has fallen for some little slapper when he's got a wife sitting at home who's lovely, and a great shag to boot... Eh? What? Have I said something wrong?

Mais tu vois pas qu'elle louche sur ton mec? T'as de la merde dans les yeux ou quoi? Je te dis qu'elle veut se le faire!
Can't you see that she's eyeing up your man? Are you blind, for God's sake? I'm telling you she wants to shag him!

Il rentra du boulot plus tôt que prévu et trouva sa bonne femme en train de se faire tirer dans le salon par le réparateur de télévisions, alors que défilait le générique des "Feux de l'amour."
He got home from work earlier than expected and found his wife getting rogered by the TV repair man in the living-room while the credits of "The Young and the Restless" were rolling.

Il a pris son pied avec la gonzesse, et ses jambes à son cou quand le mari s'est pointé.

He had got off with the woman but took to his heels when her husband turned up.

bisexual (to be): être bi, marcher à voile et à vapeur

bottom: le cul, le joufflu, le pétard, le popotin, le prose, le valseur, les miches (*fem.*)

breasts: les roberts (*masc.*), les parechocs (*masc.*), les nichons (*masc.*), les nibards (*masc.*), les nénés (*masc.*), les lolos (*masc.*), les roploplos (*masc.*)

brothel: un bobinard, un bordel, un boxon, un claque

clitoris: le bonbon, le bouton, le grain de café

condom: une capote (anglaise)

cuckold (a): un cocu

depraved person: un vicelard/une vicelarde

dirty old man: un vieux vicelard

doggy-style: en levrette

easy lay (to be an): avoir la cuisse légère, être une chaudasse

ejaculate (to): balancer la purée, décharger, juter

erection (to have an): avoir le gourdin, avoir la trique, bander, marquer midi; *to lose one's erection*: débander

eyeful (to get an): se rincer l'œil

female genitals: la chagatte, la chatte, la cramouille, la craquette, la foufoune, le millefeuille, le minou, la motte, la moule

flat-chested woman (she's a): c'est une vraie planche à repasser *or* à pain, elle est plate comme une limande

fondle (to): tripoter, palucher, peloter

French kiss (a): une galoche, un palot, un patin, une pelle; *to give somebody a French kiss*: rouler une galoche *or* un palot *or* un patin *or* une pelle à quelqu'un

get a good seeing-to (to): passer à la casserole

get off with someone (to): *(of man:)* lever une nana; *(of woman)*: lever un mec

gonorrhoea: la chtouille, la chaudepisse; *to have gonorrhoea*: être plombé

good body (to have a): être bien foutu *or* balancé
good in bed (she's): elle est bonne, c'est un bon coup
gooseberry (to play): tenir la chandelle
have sex (to): baiser, se mélanger, s'envoyer en l'air, niquer, limer; *(of man)*: tirer un coup, tirer sa chique, tremper son biscuit; *to have sex with somebody*: baiser quelqu'un, se farcir quelqu'un, s'envoyer quelqu'un, se taper quelqu'un, se payer quelqu'un; *(of man)*: tringler quelqu'un, sauter quelqu'un, troncher quelqu'un, grimper quelqu'un, bourrer quelqu'un, niquer quelqu'un, limer quelqu'un, queuter quelqu'un, fourrer quelqu'un, enfiler quelqu'un, besogner quelqu'un, mettre quelqu'un
heterosexual (a): un/une hétéro
homosexual (a): un homo, une lope, une pédale, un pédé, une tante, une tantouze, une tapette, une tarlouze, une tata; *(effeminate)*: une (grande) folle; *homosexual men*: *(collectively)* la jaquette; *to be a homosexual*: en être, être de la jaquette, être de la bagouse; *to be a passive homosexual*: en filer, donner *or* filer du rond *or* du chouette *or* du petit
leatherboy: un pédé cuir
lesbian: une brouteuse, une goudou, une gouine, une gousse
masochistic: maso
masturbate (to): se branler, se faire une branlette, se soulager; *(men only)*: se taper sur la colonne, faire cinq contre un, se palucher, se pignoler, se pogner, se polir le chinois, se taper un rassis *or* une queue, se tirer sur l'élastique; *(women only)*: s'astiquer la motte, jouer de la mandoline, se compter les poils
naked: à poil, à loilpé
neck (to): se bécoter
ogle (to): mater, reluquer, lorgner; *man who likes ogling others*: un mateur
oral sex on somebody (to perform): faire une gâterie à quelqu'un, sucer quelqu'un; *(on a woman)*: brouter le minou *or* le cresson à quelqu'un; *(on a man)*: brouter la tige à quelqu'un, faire une gourmandise *or* une pipe *or* un pompier *or* une

plume *or* une turlute à quelqu'un, pomper le dard à quelqu'un, souffler dans le poireau à quelqu'un

orgasm (to have an): prendre son pied, reluire; *(of woman only)*: mouiller

orgy: une partouze

penis: la pine, la queue, le bout, le dard, le braquemart, la bite, la teub, le nœud, le cigare à moustache

period (to be having one's): avoir ses ours *or* ses ragnagnas *or* ses Anglais

pet (to): peloter

pimp (a): un maquereau, un mac, un hareng

pubic hair: *(of female)* le barbu

rebuffed (to be): se prendre une veste, se prendre un vent, se prendre un zef, se prendre un rateau

semen: le foutre, le jute

sex: *(as an activity)* la baise, le cul

sex-mad (to be): *(of man)*: être queutard, être un chaud lapin, être chaud de la pince; *(of woman)*: avoir le feu aux fesses *or* au cul

sexual partner (a good): un bon coup, une affaire (au pieu)

shag (she needs a good): c'est une mal-baisée

shaggable: baisable, mettable

sodomize somebody (to): empaffer quelqu'un, enculer quelqu'un, taper dans la lune *or* la raie à quelqu'un

solicit (to): racoler

swallow (to): avaler la fumée

tart: une garce, une pute, une pouffe, une pouffiasse, une traînée, une salope, une roulure, une chaudasse

tease (a): une allumeuse

testicles: les bonbons *(masc.)*, les burnes *(fem.)*, les burettes *(fem.)*, les couilles *(fem.)*, les joyeuses *(fem.)*, les précieuses *(fem.)*, les roustons *(masc.)*, les valseuses *(fem.)*, les noisettes *(fem.)*

trick (a): une passe

turn gay (to): virer homo, virer sa cuti

walk the streets (to): faire le tapin *or* le trottoir, tapiner

well-hung (to be): être bien membré *or* monté

whore (a): une putain, une pute, une morue, une garce, une pouffiasse

wife-swapping party: *(between two couples)* la partie carrée

Did you know that

The word *roberts*, meaning "breasts", comes from a once-famous brand of baby bottle, and the word *braquemart*, meaning "penis", originally referred to a type of cutlass.

Test your rude French

Try and match the French sentence with its accurate English translation.

❶ Ils passent leur temps à se mélanger, ces deux-là
a) They both are very disorganized individuals
b) They spend their time getting pissed, these two
c) These two just won't stop shagging

❷ Sa frangine a la cuisse légère
a) His sister is a very good dancer
b) His sister will sleep with anybody
c) His wife is very curvaceous

❸ Il marche à voile et à vapeur
a) He's a very resourceful individual
b) He's nothing but a no-good hypocrite
c) He's bisexual

shopping

In many respects France is a shopper's paradise. Its department stores are second to none and its huge hypermarkets sell everything under the sun from dog food to car alarms, from preserved tripe to quality bilingual dictionaries, all at very competitive prices. This chapter will provide invaluable help to shopaholics and shopaphobics alike.

A few useful phrases in context

Shopping Hell

Au fur et à mesure que sa bourgeoise entassait les objets coûteux et inutiles et les fringues hors de prix dans le caddie, le pauvre mec calculait mentalement le nombre d'heures sup qu'il allait devoir se coltiner une fois de retour au burlingue.

As his other half was piling pricey but totally useless objects and extortionate clothes into the shopping trolley, the poor guy was doing a mental calculation of how many hours of overtime he'd have to put in once he was back at the office.

Le gamin insistait pour que ses vieux lui achètent le survêt de ses rêves; les parents horrifiés essayaient de le convaincre que ça ne valait pas le coup de claquer 50 euros de plus pour un vulgaire logo. Sans succès.

The kid was insisting that his old dears buy him the tracksuit he longed for. His horrified parents tried to convince him that it wasn't worth spending an extra 50 euros just for a logo. It didn't work.

Sa rombière l'a traîné de force dans les magazes quatre jours de suite. Le cinquième jour, le pauvre mec, qui pouvait plus arquer, s'est esbigné discrétos vers le rayon literie pour aller piquer un petit roupillon.

His old dear had dragged him around the shops for four days in a row. On the fifth day, the poor guy couldn't walk another step, so he discreetly buggered off to the bedding department to have a bit of a kip.

Getting ripped off

La boutique du brocanteur était un foutoir immonde rempli de saloperies qu'il fourguait à prix d'or aux touristes étrangers les moins avertis.

The second-hand dealer's shop was a disgusting shambles, full of hideous old junk that he would flog for a small fortune to unsuspecting foreign tourists.

L'angliche eut la mauvaise idée de regarder combien coûtait, chez les frenchies, le biclou qu'il avait payé la peau des fesses chez lui. Ce fut le début d'une grosse déprime.

The Brit had the bad idea of looking to see how much the Frogs were charging for the bike he'd paid an arm and a leg for back home. That marked the start of a major downer.

Tu t'es fait entuber dans les grandes largeurs! J'ai trouvé exactement le même thermomètre en forme de tour Eiffel moitié moins cher.

You've been totally ripped off! I've found exactly the same Eiffel Tower thermometer for half the price!

Embarrassment

L'exhibo avait fait exprès de ne pas boucler la lourde de la cabine d'essayage pour qu'on le "surprenne" en train d'ôter son calbute.

The flasher purposely didn't lock the door of the changing room just so that someone would "accidentally" catch him taking his pants off.

C'est au moment de se déchausser pour essayer une paire de pompes qu'il s'est rendu compte que ses fumantes étaient trouées et plutôt cradingues.

Just as he was taking his shoes off to try on another pair, he realized his socks were full of holes and hadn't been near a washing machine for weeks.

Le vendeur au sourire enjôleur réussit à la convaincre que la robe ras la touffe dans laquelle elle était boudinée comme c'est pas permis lui allait à ravir et mettait ses jambonneaux en valeur.

The sales assistant with the charming smile managed to convince her that the bum-freezer mini-skirt she was bursting out of suited her down to the ground and showed off her chunky thighs to perfection.

Alternative shopping

Il s'est pointé au comptoir avec le pack de six bibines qu'il venait d'acheter et a demandé à ce qu'on lui fasse un paquet-cadeau. "C'est pour offrir", qu'il a dit.

He went to the check-out with the six-pack of beer he'd just bought and asked for it to be gift-wrapped. "It's a present", he said.

Ce qui l'éclatait, c'était de se fringuer super classe, d'emprunter la Rolex d'un pote banquier et d'aller essayer une Porsche ou une Mercedes puis de dire au vendeur: "Remarquable, mon vieux! Si jamais un jour j'ai du pognon, c'est celle-là que je m'offrirai!"

What cracked him up was putting on some dead flash clothes, borrowing a banker friend's Rolex, going to test-drive a Porsche or a Merc and then saying to the salesman: "Great car, mate! If I ever have any cash, that's the one I'll buy!"

banknote: le biffeton, le fafiot
bowtie: le nœud pap
bra: le soutif
cap: la bâche, la gâpette
clothes: les fringues *(fem.)*, les frusques *(fem.)*, les nippes *(fem.)*
expensive: chéro, reuch; *it's expensive*: ça raque, c'est reuch, ça douille
hat: le bibi, le bitos, le galure
money: le fric, le blé, l'oseille *(fem.)*, l'artiche *(fem.)*, la t(h)une, le pognon
overcoat: le pardingue
pay (to): banquer, casquer, raquer
penniless (to be): être sans un radis, être raide comme un passe-lacet
pocket: la fouille, la profonde
purse: le crabe, le morlingue
rich (to be): être plein aux as, être pété de thunes
rip-off: une arnaque
ripped-off (to be): se faire arnaquer, se faire écorcher, se faire entuber
rubbish: la camelote
sell (to): fourguer
shirt: la liquette, la limace
shoes: les croquenots *(masc.)*, les godasses *(fem.)*, les godillots *(masc.)*, les grolles *(fem.)*, les pompes *(fem.)*
shopaholic: un/une accro du shopping
sleeveless vest: le marcel
small change: la ferraille, la mitraille
socks: les fumantes *(fem.)*
spend (to): casquer, claquer
suit: le costard
ten thousand French francs: *(formerly)* le bâton, la brique, la patate, l'unité *(fem.)*
tie: une étrangleuse
tracksuit: le survêt
trousers: le bénard, le falzar, le futal, le fute, le froc
underpants: le calbar, le calbute, le calcif, le slibar

very expensive (to be): coûter les yeux de la tête,
coûter la peau des fesses, coûter bonbon
very short: *(of skirt, dress)* ras la touffe
wallet: le larfeuille

Did you know that

Even though the French franc ceased to
be legal tender in France in 2002 as it was
replaced by the euro, some shops still give
prices in francs as well as in euros (for
reference only) as many people haven't fully
adjusted to the new currency. When referring
to the value of very expensive things, such
as property, it is therefore common for
people still to talk in francs. The situation
is further complicated by the fact that some
older people still think in terms of "anciens
francs" (old francs), which were replaced
by the "nouveau franc" (new franc) in 1960,
one new franc being worth 100 old francs.
However, slang terms specifically related to
the euro have yet to emerge.

Test your rude French

Try and match the sentence in French with its accurate English
translation.

❶ **Il ne lui reste que de la ferraille**
a) He only has cheap jewellery left in stock
b) His car is a write-off
c) He's only got small change left

❷ Il s'est acheté une nouvelle limace

a) He bought a new pet slug

b) He bought a new shirt

c) He bought a new – albeit very slow – car

❸ Elle est complètement raide; elle a claqué tout ce qu'elle avait

a) She says her back and legs are feeling very stiff and that she must have pulled every muscle in her body

b) She's completely drunk and I think she spilled the beans

c) She's completely skint; she's down to her last penny

work

"Le travail c'est la santé, rien faire c'est la conserver" goes the song. But for those who weren't born in the leisured classes – and there are many – work is still a necessary evil. One good way of relieving the tedium inherent in most jobs is to look for employment abroad and widen one's horizons. Jobs may not be as plentiful in France as in the UK, but if you do manage to find employment there, you'll probably enjoy a shorter working week than in Blighty, more protection and better benefits as well as many more bank holidays. And if you're unhappy about your working conditions you can always go on strike or take to the streets. Having said that, don't expect to be twiddling your thumbs the rest of the time: it's not for nothing that the productivity rate in France is one of the highest in the world. At any rate this section will enable you to boost your street cred with your fellow workers. Au boulot!

A few useful phrases in context

Looking for a job

J'ai plus un rond, j'ai déjà tapé du fric à tous mes potes: il y a pas à tortiller, il faut que je cherche du taf.
I'm totally skint and I've already scrounged money off all my mates. There are no two ways about it, I'm going to have to look for a job.

Un copain qu'a le bras long lui a promis qu'il lui trouverait un boulot vraiment pépère au syndicat d'initiative de La Courneuve. C'est chouette d'avoir du piston!
Some friend of his who's got plenty of clout promised he'd find him a cushy little job in the tourist office at La Courneuve. It's great to have friends in the right places!

J'angoisse à mort: j'ai un rancard demain pour un super job dans un fast-food; j'ai intérêt à assurer.
I'm in a complete flap – I've an interview tomorrow for a brilliant job in a fast-food restaurant. I'd better do OK.

C'est pas le genre à se casser le tronc: il attend que tout lui tombe tout cuit dans le bec.
He's not the type to put himself out: he's just waiting for everything to fall into his lap.

Having a job

Le taulier m'a à la bonne depuis que je lui lèche les bottes; j'espère prendre rapidement du galon.
I've been in the boss's good books ever since I started brown-nosing him; I hope to get promoted soon.

Votre augmentation, vous pouvez vous asseoir dessus, mettez-vous bien ça dans le crâne!
You can forget any hope of getting a pay rise; get that into your head!

On the way out

Je me suis fait souffler dans les bronches par le patron; il m'a reproché d'être toujours à la bourre et d'avoir un poil dans la main.
I got bawled out by the boss – he slated me for always being late and for being bone idle.

Démerdard comme il est, je suis sûr qu'il va se faire des couilles en or dans sa nouvelle boîte.
Knowing a trick or two as he does, I'm sure he'll make a packet in his new company.

Tous ses collègues de burlingue lui tirent dans les pattes et le chef l'a dans le pif: il va pas faire de vieux os ici.
All his colleagues are giving him a hard time and the boss can't stand the sight of him: he's not going to last long here.

Le patron m'a dans le collimateur depuis qu'il m'a chopé en train de faire une photocopie de mes fesses. Je crois que je me suis définitivement grillé.
The boss has been keeping tabs on me since he caught me photocopying my arse. I think I've definitely had it this time.

Quand le boss lui a fait remarquer qu'il se barrait en avance alors qu'il était arrivé à la bourre, il lui a répondu que, justement, il voulait pas être en retard deux fois dans la même journée.

When the boss pointed out to him that he was leaving early and yet he hadn't got in on time, he replied that that was just it, he didn't want to be late twice in the same day.

J'en ai marre de vos excuses à deux balles: hier vous vous faites enlever par des extra-terrestres, passe encore; mais votre histoire de train qui tombe en rade, franchement, n'espérez pas me faire avaler vos salades!
I've had it up to here with your lame excuses; yesterday you get abducted by aliens, fair enough, but your story that the train broke down, I mean really, don't expect me to believe your lies!

Looking for new challenges elsewhere

Deux minutes de pause-pipi le matin, un quart d'heure pour casser la graine et pas le droit de causer avec les potes: c'est le bagne ici! C'est décidé, je rends mon tablier.
We're only allowed two minutes to go for a pee in the morning and a quarter of an hour to grab a bite to eat, and chatting to your mates is banned – it's like a sweatshop here! That's it, I'm handing in my notice.

C'est pas que je les aie à la retourne, mais je tiens pas à continuer à bosser comme un nègre et être payé au lance-pierre; autant toucher le chômedu.
It's not that I'm bone idle or anything but I can't be doing with slogging my guts out for peanuts – I might as well be on the dole.

Mais qu'ils me virent si ça les amuse! Je vais pas faire la pute pour un boulot de sous-fifre!
Oh let them kick me out if that's what they want! I'm not going to brown-nose them to let me work as a complete dogsbody.

Vous pouvez défaire les valoches: je viens de me faire virer, alors on peut faire une croix sur les vacances.
You can unpack the suitcases: I've just been given the boot, so we can wave goodbye to going on holiday.

ambitious (to be): avoir les dents longues, en vouloir

appointment: le rancard

behind with one's work (to be): être à la bourre

blunder: la boulette

boss: le boss, le taulier

brown-nose (to): faire de la lèche, faire la pute; *to brown-nose somebody*: cirer les pompes à quelqu'un, lécher les bottes à quelqu'un, passer de la pommade à quelqu'un

competent (to be): assurer (un max)

company: la boîte, la boutique

computer: un ordi

couldn't-care-less attitude: le je-m'en-foutisme

crash (to): *(of computer)* planter

cushy job: le boulot pépère, la planque

dawdle (to): lambiner

dole (to be on the): être au chômedu

down and out (to be): être dans la dèche *or* dans la mouise

exert oneself (to): mouiller sa chemise *or* sa liquette, se casser le tronc

exploit the workforce (to): faire suer le burnous

fire (to): balancer, sacquer, vider, virer

go-getter: le battant; *(young)*: le jeune loup

have it in for somebody (to): avoir quelqu'un dans le nez *or* le pif

incompetent person: un jeanfoutre, un branleur, un gugusse, un guignol

influential (to be): avoir le bras long

late (to be): être à la bourre

laze about (to): buller, ne pas en foutre une rame, ne pas en ramer une, glander, glandouiller

lazy (to be): avoir les côtes en long, les avoir à la retourne, les avoir palmées, avoir un poil dans la main

like somebody (to): avoir quelqu'un à la bonne

make an enemy of somebody (to): se mettre quelqu'un à dos

manual worker: le pue-la-sueur

mess things up (to): cafouiller

mint (to make a): se faire un fric fou, s'en mettre plein les poches, se faire des couilles en or

money: le fric, le blé, l'oseille *(fem.)*, l'artiche *(fem.)*, la t(h)une, le pognon, la maille

moonlight (to): travailler au black

office: le burlingue

out of one's depth (to be): être (complètement) largué, ne pas faire le poids

pencil-pusher: le grattepapier, le rond-de-cuir

presentable (to look): bien présenter, être propre sur soi

promoted (to be): prendre du galon

resign (to): rendre son tablier, plaquer son boulot

resourceful: démerdard

right people (to know the): avoir du piston

routine: le train-train; *routine of the commuter:* métro, boulot, dodo

run somebody down (to): casser du sucre sur le dos de quelqu'un, tirer dans les pattes à quelqu'un, débiner quelqu'un

skiver: le tire-au-flanc, le tire-au-cul, le glandeur

slave-driver: le négrier

slog away (to): bosser comme un nègre, se décarcasser, en mettre un coup

supervisor (petty and tyrannical): le chefaillon

talk shop (to): parler boutique

tell somebody off (to): souffler dans les bronches à quelqu'un, passer un savon à quelqu'un, remonter les bretelles à quelqu'un, taper sur les doigts à quelqu'un

underling: le sous-fifre

underpay (to): payer au lance-pierre

watch somebody closely (to): avoir quelqu'un dans le collimateur

whipping boy: le souffre-douleur

work: le boulot, le taf, le turbin

work (to): bosser, boulonner, bûcher, marner, trimer, turbiner, gratter

Did you know that

The expression *faire suer le burnous* meaning "to exploit one's workforce" comes from the colonial period when French settlers in North Africa used to work their native labourers very hard; a *burnous* is a type of garment worn by Arabs.

Test your rude French

Try and match the French sentence with its accurate English translation.

❶ **Qu'est-ce qu'elle en veut, la secrétaire! Elle a les dents tellement longues qu'elles rayent le parquet**

a) The secretary's indefatigable! She insists on working even though she's way past retirement age

b) The secretary really wants to get ahead. She's incredibly ambitious

c) The secretary has a chip on her shoulder. She's always snarling at everybody

❷ **Ce qu'elle peut être rasoir, elle est toujours en train de parler boutique!**

a) She's dead sharp but the only thing she ever talks about is shopping

b) She's not a great conversationalist and besides she's got a one-track mind

c) She's a real bore, she's always talking shop

❸ **Il a le bras long mais ça ne l'empêche pas d'avoir un poil dans la main**

a) He might be able to pull strings but he's a lazy bugger all the same

b) He's long-limbed but he's as hairy as an ape

c) He's both a control freak and a compulsive masturbator

A Look at French Slang, or "Argot"

The term "argot" first appeared in writing in 1628 in a book called *Le Jargon de l'argot*, when it was used to designate professional beggars and thieves collectively. During the 17th century there was a shift in meaning and by 1690 the word no longer applied to beggars and thieves but to their secret language. But this is not to say that this type of language did not exist before the emergence of the term "argot".

the first known glossary of French slang was compiled by the police in 1455 during the trial of some bandits

As a matter of fact, the first known glossary of French slang was compiled by the police in 1455 during the trial of the bandits known as the "Coquillards" (the poet François Villon is said to have been a member of the Coquillards and he used slang in his writings). Some of the terms featured in this glossary have survived to this day, such as the term *quille* meaning "leg". Others have changed only slightly, such as the word "*enterver*", now *entrave*r, which means "to understand", as in *j'entrave que dalle* ("I understand bugger all"). Other words, like *dupe*, have since completely lost their slang connotations. On the other hand, a word like *pisser* ("to piss" – yes, this most English of words comes from the French), dating back at least to the Middle Ages, only became vulgar and objectionable during the 19th century.

Interestingly, some scholars have argued that the Coquillards were not in fact using a cryptic language as such, but merely a form of dialectal and uneducated speech that was unknown to people of higher social status. But whether intentionally or accidentally, a type of unconventional language emerged that served as a coded language for criminals, who used it so as not to be understood by other people. Unsurprisingly, the authorities have always taken a keen interest in crime slang and it is no accident that someone like François Eugène Vidocq (1775–1857), a famous policeman and slang specialist (who served as a model for the character Vautrin in Balzac's novels), was himself a reformed criminal.

Trade jargons

But the word "argot" doesn't belong exclusively to the world of crime. Indeed, many trades spawn their own jargons that go well beyond the requirements of purely technical terminology, and these are also referred to as "argot". A good example of this is "louchébem" or butchers' slang, a type of slang formed by replacing the initial consonant of a word with the letter "l" and moving the original consonant to the end of the word, followed by the syllable "em" (the word "louchébem" is itself the result of this procedure applied to the word "boucher"). Any word can be transformed using this code-language, even the most ordinary. The main purpose of this type of slang is not to avoid police detection (even though some might argue that meat is murder) but to create a sort of complicity between members of a given group by being deliberately unintelligible to outsiders. This is more or less the role fulfilled by *verlan* (or backslang) for today's teenagers (of which more later).

> the main purpose is to create a sort of complicity between members of a given group

Of course, crime slang and the "in-house" slang used by people working within a specific trade or profession often overlap. This is obvious in the field of prostitution, for instance, where each category of prostitute used to have (and probably still has) its own name. For instance, the *équarrisseuse* (from "équarrir", meaning "to quarter") was a prostitute who used to operate near abattoirs; prostitutes working in bars are called *échassières* (from "échassier", meaning "a wader", a type of bird characterized by its long legs) because they are often perched on bar stools. Those who operate in parks and trains are called *bucoliques* and *waggonières* respectively, while those who solicit from their cars are *amazones* (because they never leave their cars, just as the mythical female warriors were always on horseback) and their humbler streetwalking sisters are known as *piétonnières*. At the very bottom of the pecking order is the *paillasson*, or "doormat". (As Jonathon Green, the English slang specialist, once wrote: "slang is as it is and what it is is largely cruel. (...) It is no comforter.")

A hybrid language

In common parlance the word "argot" no longer refers exclusively to crime slang or to slang used by a particular professional group but to a type of uneducated speech that used to be spoken by the populace of big cities (chiefly in Paris and its surroundings) up until a few decades ago. Actually, it can be argued that "argot" is a predominantly Parisian linguistic phenomenon. Tellingly, Louis Barthas, a First World War soldier from southern France, wrote the following about his first visit to Paris in his now famous diaries*: "le lendemain, (...) je débarquais à Paris, Paname, comme disaient les poilus parisiens qui n'appellent rien par leur vrai nom" ("the next morning I arrived in Paris, or 'Paname' as the Parisian *poilus* – who never call things by their proper names – used to say").

Paris has always been France's melting pot, and over a long period of time some words and expressions used by people from the provinces, tradesmen and criminals were amalgamated to form this new type of language. Foreigners and travellers also contributed to French slang: for example, *une gouape* ("a thug") comes from the Spanish "guapo", *schpile* (meaning "game") comes from the German "Spiel", *schlass* (meaning "knife") comes from the English "slash", and the word *grisbi* ("money") is said to come from the English "crispy" (supposedly because of the crispness of new banknotes).

Main characteristics

One of the most striking features of French slang is the range of its vocabulary. Even though it is in the fields of sex, bodily functions, drunkenness, madness, money, violence and crime that "argot" is at its most prolific, there exist slang terms for many thoroughly mundane items. For instance, the word "parapluie" (umbrella) has no fewer than three slang equivalents: *le pébroque, le pépin* and *le riflard*; there are more than a

> sex, bodily functions, drunkenness, madness, money, violence and crime

---

*Les carnets de guerre de Louis Barthas, tonnelier, 1914–1918 (published by La Découverte).

dozen words for "shoes" (the most common ones being *les godasses, les pompes, les grolles*), and the word "bed" has about a dozen slang equivalents, including *le paddock, le plumard* and *le pucier*.

Even very matter-of-fact things can be expressed in argot thanks to its extensive vocabulary. Sentences as banal as, for instance, "he was late for his appointment" and "she opened the door and turned the light on" have their equivalents in argot: "il s'est pointé à la bourre à son rancard" and "elle a ouvert la lourde et allumé la loupiote", respectively.

Word formation

Countless slang words are created by dropping the ends (or much more rarely the beginnings) of words and adding more or less bizarre endings. That's how "le bureau" (office) becomes *le burlingue*, "la bouteille" (bottle) becomes *la boutanche*, "la valise" (suitcase) turns into *la valoche*, and "le cinéma" is known as *le cinoche*. Dozens of words are created by simply adding an "o" to a truncated word, as in *alcolo* (from "alcoolique"), *apéro* (from "apéritif"), *proprio* (from "propriétaire"), *frigo* (from "frigidaire") or *projo* (from "projecteur").

Often, a slang word is obtained by focusing on one of the main characteristics of the thing described (or at least perceived as such in the twisted world of slang). That's why a bed is *un pucier* (because it's full of "puces" or fleas), a door is *une lourde* ("a heavy one"), a comb is *un crasseux* (meaning "a filthy one"), a tongue is *une menteuse* (meaning "a liar", because that's the organ people use to talk and therefore to lie with), and the posterior is *le gagne-pain* (because it is the part of the body some people use to make a living). In old slang, *le Sénat* (the Senate, the upper house of the French Parliament) came to be used to refer to a dosshouse for retired prostitutes because of the advanced age of the members of both institutions.

Other slang words and expressions originate through colourful metaphors. For instance, *les portugaises* means "the ears" because of a type of oyster called "la portugaise" whose shape is reminiscent of that of an ear. The metaphor can be extended by saying "il a les portugaises ensablées" ("he's got sand in his ears/ oysters") when talking about anyone who is hard of hearing.

slang words and expressions originate through colourful metaphors

Le papillon (literal meaning "butterfly") is the parking ticket that a traffic warden sticks underneath a driver's windscreen wiper, where it flutters in the wind; also, people can collect either kind of "papillons", butterflies or parking tickets.

Lâcher la rampe or *la bouée* ("to let go of the handrail/the buoy") means "to die", and *bouffer les pissenlits par la racine* ("to eat dandelions from the roots"), which is almost identical to the English "to push up the daisies", means "to be dead".

In the world of slang, *le coupe-cigare* (literally "cigar cutter") is an implement that everyone possesses and serves to cut a rather peculiar type of cigar: it means "anus". *Le chauve à col roulé* ("the bald man in a polo neck jumper") refers to the male member, and in a similar vein, both *faire sauter la cervelle à Charles-le-Chauve* ("to blow Charles the Bald's brains out") and *étrangler le borgne* ("to strangle the one-eyed man") refer to male masturbation for reasons that need no explaining.

When applied to a clock, the expression *marquer midi* means "to show 12 o'clock" but when applied to a man it takes on an altogether different meaning "namely to have an erection" (of course, the expression becomes totally irrelevant if one pictures a digital clock...).

Les Anglais ont débarqué ("the English have landed") is an interesting historical metaphor that harks back to the times when France and Britain were almost continuously at war with each other: it means "to have one's period" (on account of the red uniforms of British soldiers).

The feline metaphor used to designate female genitals exists in French as well as in English with *chatte, minou, minet, minette* (all meaning "pussy"). Finally, if one wants to comment on someone's stinginess, one can use the expression *il a des oursins dans le morlingue* (which means literally "he's got sea urchins in his wallet"), an expression which very vividly and colourfully conveys someone's reluctance to put his hand in his pocket.

Playing on words

Humour plays a very important part in the formation of slang words and expressions, as we've seen with some of the items mentioned above. Numerous slang words or expressions are created by taking perfectly ordinary language items and distorting their meaning.

This is how, in the field of prostitution, *les bancs de Terre-Neuve* came to take on a peculiar meaning: these were originally the waters of Newfoundland where cod used to be plentiful; once you know that the French for "cod" is *morue* and that this word also means "whore" in slang, then you can begin to see why this expression was used to refer to some Parisian boulevards where there used to be many streetwalkers. It is worth noting that for some reason the slang of prostitution is very fish-orientated: a pimp is *un maquereau* ("mackerel") or *un hareng* ("herring").

In printing, *être sous presse* means "to be in the press", but when talking about a prostitute it changes its meaning to "to be busy with a client". In the slang of shopkeepers, *une blanchisseuse* (literally "a laundrywoman") is a person who leaves

> for some reason the slang of prostitution is very fish-orientated

without buying anything but promises that they'll be back: that is because they say "je repasserai" as they leave, and "repasser" means both "to call again" and "to iron". Similarly, in slang *un archéologue* ("an archaeologist") designates a pickpocket. Why? "Simply" because (i) archaeologists do excavations ("faire des fouilles" in French); (ii) the word *fouille* also means "pocket" in slang; and (iii) "faire les poches à quelqu'un" means "to pick somebody's pockets". In other words, the job description of an archaeologist phrased in normal parlance is the same as that of a pickpocket in slang. The expression "se décalcifier" works in an almost identical way: its original meaning ("to lose calcium") is medical, but since the word *calcif* is slang for "underpants", the temptation of completely distorting a respectable scientific term proved too great for some and it came to mean "to remove one's underpants" in slang.

Some slang words are formed through very simple (and rather silly) puns: a concierge is called *un cloporte* ("a woodlouse") because his job is to close doors ("il clôt les portes") and *un lancelot* is a fireman because he sprays water ("il lance l'eau"). Some other puns are strokes of genius: for instance, in what language apart from French is there a slang term meaning "annoyed by one's mother-in-law"? The term in question is *embellemerdé*, a blend of *belle-mère* ("mother-in-law") and *emmerdé* ("annoyed"). Finally, still in the puns department, a relatively recent slang synonym for "cigarette" is worth mentioning, namely *nuit grave*, where *nuit* has nothing to do with "night" but everything to do with the verb *nuire* ("to harm"). The coinage derives from the health warning on French packets of cigarettes: "*nuit gravement à la santé*" ("smoking can seriously damage your health").

"Verlan" and recent trends in argot

No article about French slang would be complete without a few words about *verlan*. This code-language is formed by inverting the syllables of words and making any spelling changes necessary to aid pronunciation. The word *verlan* is itself the inverted form of "l'envers" ("back to front"). Some *verlan* terms have passed into spoken French generally and are used or understood by a great many speakers, eg *laisse béton* (*laisse tomber*: "forget it") – popularized by the singer Renaud – *ripou* ("a bent copper", from *pourri*: "rotten") and *meuf* (*femme*: "woman").

Any word can, in theory, be turned into *verlan*. For instance: *pétard* ("a joint") becomes *tarpé, bizarre* becomes *zarbi, pute* ("whore") becomes *teupu*, which is then shortened to *teup*. Words of only one syllable can also be "verlanized," eg *chaud* becomes *auch*; an "e" is frequently added to aid pronunciation, eg *flic* becomes *keufli*, which is shortened to *keuf, mère* becomes *reumè*, which is in turn shortened to *reum*. A term may be "verlanized" twice – the term *rebeu*, for example, comes from the verlan for "Arabe", *beur*, which is then "re-verlanized" to give *rebeu*.

Verlan is an extremely generative form of slang. Though it has always existed, it has become incredibly popular with the young over the last twenty years or so, and it accounts for the vast majority of words used in "l'argot des cités", also known as "l'argot des banlieues", which is a type of slang spoken by young people in the underprivileged areas on the periphery of large cities (mainly Paris).

"L'argot des cités" is noticeably different from the more traditional type of slang that used to be spoken up until thirty or thirty-five years ago. It has kept a number of terms from that traditional slang but, as we've seen, it has added a great many *verlan* words as well as English words (mainly from American rap songs) and terms from Arabic (this is because of the big influx of immigrants from North Africa after the Second World War, when France needed labour for its expanding economy). "L'argot des cités" has had considerable media coverage over the past few years because of endemic unrest and riots in some deprived areas, and also through films like Mathieu Kassovitz's

> The word *verlan* is itself the inverted form of "l'envers"

La Haine in 1995. It has even been the subject of scholarly works and dictionaries by some eminent linguists. However, it is hard to tell if this type of "argot" has any future beyond the areas where young people use it. Even though it is used by many French rap artists, it has so far failed to acquire a status in literature or cinema or even poetry in the way traditional slang did.

A Quick Glance at Slang in Literature

"Argot" has been a source of inspiration and fascination for many writers, including some of the giants of French literature.

Hugo's "pustulous vocabulary"

In a section devoted to slang in *Les Misérables*, **Victor Hugo** (1802–1885) described this language as "that abject dialect which is dripping with filth, that pustulous vocabulary each word of which seems an unclean ring from a monster of the mire and the shadows. (...) It seems, in fact, to be a sort of horrible beast made for the night which has just been torn from its cesspool. (...) Slang (...) is nothing other (...) than the homely, uneasy, crafty, treacherous, venomous, cruel, equivocal, vile, profound, fatal tongue of wretchedness." Hardly a ringing endorsement for slang as literary material...

But a few paragraphs later he writes: "slang, whether the public admit the fact or not, has its syntax and its poetry. It is a language." Hugo's attitude to slang is ambivalent; it is one of fascination combined with revulsion, but overall fascination seems to dominate and he does use many slang terms in *Les Misérables* to add some local colour to his dialogues. It has since been shown that many of Hugo's observations about the origin of slang words are inaccurate and that he had actually

> ...slang, whether the public admit the fact or not, has its syntax and its poetry. It is a language.
>
> VICTOR HUGO

coined a substantial number of words himself. This in itself can be seen as a testimony to slang as a creative and liberating medium in literature.

Balzac's "subterranean world"

The novelist **Honoré de Balzac** (1799–1850), another titan of French letters (pun accidental), was also very interested in slang. One section of *Splendeurs et misères des courtisanes* (A Harlot High and Low) is actually entitled *Philosophical, Linguistic and Literary Essay on Slang, Prostitution and Thieves*. In it he writes: "there is no more energetic or colourful language than that of this subterranean world. (...) Each word of this language is a brutal, ingenious or fearful image. (...) Everything is savage in this idiom. (...) And what poetry! (...) What vivacity in these images!"

Throughout *Splendeurs et misères des courtisanes*, he uses and explains the meaning of many terms of crime slang. For instance, he explains that "the armed constabulary had a variety of cant names: on the tracks of a thief he was a *marchand de lacets*, a corruption of *maréchaussée* 'or marshalsea; (...) when taking a man to the scaffold he became a 'guillotine hussar'". Balzac uses slang for the sake of realism but he is always careful to explain the meaning of slang words to the reader.

Slang later became a staple of realist and naturalist literature. **Émile Zola** (1840–1902) also used it in his novels, but like Balzac and Hugo he wasn't a native speaker of slang. Their knowledge of slang was often based on what they found in books.

Barbusse and the slang of the trenches

Military service and indeed war were often opportunities for authors of middle-class origin to come into direct contact with slang. **Raymond Queneau** (1903–1976), the author of *Zazie dans le métro*, admitted that he only became acquainted with slang during his military service.

In his chronicle of trench warfare *Le Feu* (Under Fire), **Henri Barbusse** (1873–1935) wrote: "we've all come to speak the same language, a blend of words and expressions from jargons spoken by people from different trades, army slang, regional dialects, plus a few new coinages thrown in for good measure. This language is like a cement that binds the multitudes of men who, for many months, have come from all over France and gathered in the North-East."

For Barbusse, the presence of slang in his writing is a proof of authenticity, a guarantee that his portrayal of life in the trenches is accurate. This is made very clear in a passage where a fellow soldier observes him writing his diaries:

- Si tu fais parler les troufions dans ton livre, est-ce que tu les f'ras parler comme ils parlent, ou bien est-ce que tu arrangeras ça, en lousdoc. C'est rapport aux gros mots qu'on dit. (...) Si tu ne le dis pas, ton portrait ne sera pas r'ssemblant: c'est comme qui dirait qu'tu voudrais les peindre et que tu n'mettes pas une des couleurs les plus voyantes partout où elle est. Mais pourtant ça s'fait pas.
- Je mettrai les gros mots à leur place, mon petit père, parce que c'est la vérité.

- *If you're gonna have ordinary soldiers talking in your book, are you gonna make them talk like they really talk or are you gonna make it sound all nice and pretty? The reason I'm asking is because of the swear words we use. (...) If they're not in, it's not going to be like real life: it would be like painting the soldiers but changing some of the colours because they're too loud. But still, you don't get swear words in books.*
- *I'll put the swear words where they belong, mate, because I want to tell it like it is.*

Boudard, Le Breton and the class divide

Among the writers who contributed to popularizing slang in literature after World War II, **Alphonse Boudard** (1925–2000) and **Auguste Le Breton** (1913–1999) are worth mentioning, because, unlike authors such as Queneau, both came from the working class, both had links with the world of crime and both were native speakers of slang. Whereas Queneau used slang as literary and sometimes poetical material and loved playing on words (for instance in *Zazie dans le métro*, Zazie's uncle is a drag artist, and Queneau plays on the word "tonton" (uncle) and "tata", meaning "aunt" in normal language but "homosexual" in slang), Boudard and Le Breton regarded slang as more than a collection of words with which to spice up one's writings. To them slang grew out of the experience of the poor.

> it has lost most of its relevance since the toffs in their fine houses have become so keen on it
> AUGUSTE LE BRETON

In his dictionary of slang called *L'Argot chez les vrais de vrai*, Auguste le Breton speaks of "the people from the working classes, the people who invented slang" and says: "[slang] has lost most of its relevance since the toffs in their fine houses have become so keen on it".

For the upper classes, using slang is the linguistic equivalent of slumming it or enjoying a bit of rough. But there's little in it for the people to whom slang really belongs. The educated classes may venture into slang territory for cheap thrills at their leisure but the slang-speaking underclasses or uneducated classes don't get a look in when it comes to the language of the ruling classes. This is why many people of modest origin for whom slang is a living language feel deeply resentful when outsiders attempt to mimic them and appropriate their language, be it in an attempt to win them over ("I'm your friend, look, I speak your language!") or in an attempt to acquire some street cred.

Alphonse Boudard writes the following in his novel *Cinoche* (1974), in a passage where some cinema producers are fascinated by him because he's an ex-con:

There is no point speaking slang with all these jerks, it isn't nor shall it ever be their language. As soon as they start using a word they spoil it and it's no good any more, they murder it with their posh accents.

Similarly, the same point is outlined by **Marcel Aymé** (1902–1967) in his 1947 novel *Uranus*, in a passage where Jourdain, a young teacher from a bourgeois background, is talking to Gaigneux, a fellow communist who firmly belongs to the working class:

- d'accord, mais faut pas se gourrer...
- faut pas quoi? demanda Gaigneux en feignant de n'avoir pas compris, car il supportait mal que Jourdain s'exprimât en argot ou même dans un langage un peu peuple.
Il est vrai que le jeune professeur, lorsqu'il s'efforçait ainsi de communier plus étroitement avec le prolétariat, avait l'air d'un colonel qui goûte la soupe des simples soldats.

- OK, but we'd better make bloody sure that we're not making a cock-up!
- That we're not what? Gaigneux asked, pretending that he hadn't understood, for he found it quite irritating when Jourdain tried to speak slang or even tried to speak like a working man. It has to be said that whenever he was trying to empathize with the working class, the young teacher looked like a colonel tasting the food served to ordinary soldiers.

To Le Breton and Boudard, the poor are the rightful owners of slang and they cannot tolerate it when outsiders try to appropriate it. Le Breton writes: "when one reads the works of certain writers, one can tell immediately that they got their material from books, instead of picking up slang in the street, which is the only place where one can truly learn it" (in *L'Argot chez les vrais de vrai*).

Ironically, through the novels, glossaries and dictionaries that they published, Le Breton and Boudard largely contributed to bringing slang to the very people they were criticizing. Indeed, Le Breton's novels often look as though he did his best to cram in as many slang terms as possible, as in the following passage, which would be all but incomprehensible to many without a glossary:

> Depuis la guerre, les cinq Maltais avaient mis la pogne sur les putains de la ville, où ils régnaient en maîtres. La nuit, après les heures de tapin, ils allaient sur le tas chercher les Julies qu'ils chargeait dans leurs Rolls comme dans un autobus. Lorsqu'une pute maquée avec un hareng français les gênait, ils expédiaient une de leurs nanas pour corriger la récalcitrante. Ils ne se mouillaient pas eux-mêmes. Pas si fous. Leurs putes mettaient les autres sœurs au pli: à coups de razif. Comme les Bics. (from *Du rififi chez les hommes*, 1953)

> *Since the war, the Maltese gang had acquired the monopoly on the prostitution racket in the entire city. Late at night, after the girls had finished working, they would go round and pick them up in their Rollers, herding them in as though they were packing them into a bus. When a whore insisted on staying with her French pimp, they would send one of their girls to punish her. They didn't get their hands dirty. They knew much better than that. It was their whores who would teach the other girls a lesson: with a razor blade. Just like the Arabs.*

Céline and the slang of hatred

Of all 20th-century French writers, **Louis-Ferdinand Céline** (1894–1961) is probably the one who used slang to greatest effect in his novels. He was from a very humble background and slang was therefore not a foreign language to him, but he didn't use it to prove his working-class credentials, to show off or merely to add local colour to his writings.

Céline makes the most of the shifts in register that slang allows. With him, slang becomes a remarkably expressive language that conveys feelings of rage, frustration, alienation and hatred. As a matter of fact, Céline once said that "slang was born out of hatred". This is examplified in the following excerpt from his 1932 novel *Voyage au bout de la nuit* (Journey to the End of the Night) where a soldier tells the narrator how he had to run for his life because he was under fire:

> slang was born out of hatred
> LOUIS-FERDINAND CÉLINE

C'est maintenant ou jamais qu'il faut que tu les mettes, que je me suis dit!... Pas vrai? J'ai donc pris par le long d'un petit bois et puis là, figure-toi que j'ai rencontré notre capitaine. Il était appuyé à un arbre, bien amoché, le piston!... En train de crever qu'il était ... (...) Il saignait de partout en roulant des yeux... Y'avait personne avec lui. Il avait son compte... "Maman, maman!" qu'il pleurnichait tout en crevant et en pissant du sang aussi... "Finis ça! que je lui dis. Maman! Elle t'emmerde!"... Comme ça, dis donc, en passant!... Sur le coin de la gueule!... Tu parles si ça a dû le faire jouir la vache! Hein, vieux!... C'est pas souvent, hein, qu'on peut lui dire ce qu'on pense, au capitaine... Faut en profiter.

It's now or never I says to myself... This is the time to get going... Right? So I started through a little clump of woods and pretty soon, what do you know, I ran into our captain... he's leaning against a tree, in very bad shape!... Dying!... (...) Bleeding all over and rolling his eyes... There was nobody with him. He was through... "Mama! Mama!" he was snivelling, all the while dying and bleeding like a stuck pig. "Shut up!" I tell him. "Mama! Mama! Fuck your mama"... Just like that, on my way past, just like a kick in the teeth!... I bet that made him feel good, the bastard!... What do you think of that!... It's not every day that you can tell the captain what you think... Too good to miss...

Humour is central to Céline's style and he often uses slang to great comical effect, as in a passage in *Mort à crédit* (Death on credit), where he describes people being sick during a cross-Channel trip in almost apocalyptic terms:

Une passagère débouline*... Elle vadrouille jusque sur maman... Elle se cale pour mieux dégueuler... Un petit clebs aussi rapplique, rendu si malade qu'il en foire dans les jupons (...) Des chiottes on

---

* a coinage by Céline: it is a mixture of "débouler" (to emerge suddenly) and "dégouliner" (to drip).

pousse des cris horribles... C'est les quatre personnes qui sont bouclées qui peuvent plus vomir du tout, ni pisser, ni chiader non plus (...) Elles implorent qu'on les assassine... Et le rafiot cabre encore plus... toujours plus raide, il replonge... il se renfonce dans l'abîme.

A woman comes staggering up... she wedges herself in beside Mama so as to throw up better... There's a sick mutt, too, so sick he shits on the ladies' skirts... (...) Piercing screams are heard from the shithouse... Those four are still jammed in, they can't puke anymore, they can't pee, they can't shit... (...) They bellow, begging someone to shoot them... And the tub pitches still higher... steeper than ever... and plunges into the depths.

Céline has had many imitators but he remains unique in French literature.

Nowadays, slang is mainly used by crime writers; it is still a form of language appreciated by authors wishing to signal that their characters/narrators are street- and worldly-wise. But there is no denying that the golden age of slang in literature now seems well and truly over.

RUDE

French Humour

Here is a selection of jokes and riddles designed to help you test your knowledge of French slang and, hopefully, tickle your funny bone in the process. Actually, they may not all be hilariously funny (and some of them are decidedly un-PC) but they're all language-related and most of them play on the different meanings of a word. The corniest and most innocuous ones were originally printed in the wrappers of candy bars called *Carambar*, from the seventies onwards, and are much appreciated by schoolchildren (as well as by nostalgic grown-ups).

We have translated all the jokes and riddles into English to help the reader, but the crucial bits are often untranslatable as they usually involve some wordplay that cannot be conveyed in English. Explanations of puns and wordplay are therefore given after the translation and indicated by an arrow. The reader is encouraged to try and figure out the jokes in French before resorting to the translations and explanations.

■ Crude Crosswords

Dans un compartiment de train, il y a trois personnes : un militaire, un grand-père et sa petite fille de huit ans. Le grand-père et la fillette font chacun des mots croisés. Le grand-père demande au militaire:
- J'ai presque toutes les lettres, et pourtant je ne trouve pas. La définition est "se vide quand on tire un coup" et ça se termine par OUILLE. Vous avez une idée?
- Oui, répond le militaire, je ne connais que ça : c'est une DOUILLE. Alors la fillette:
- Zut! Papi, tu peux me passer la gomme?!

Three people are sitting in a train compartment: a soldier, an old man, and his eight-year-old granddaughter. Both the old man and his granddaughter are doing crossword puzzles. The old man says to the soldier:
- "I have almost all the letters for this one but I can't find the word. The definition is 'loses its contents when a shot is fired', and the ending is OUILLE. Any ideas?"
- "Yes", says the soldier, "it's right up my street: the word is 'douille'".
- So the little girl exclaims: "Damn! Can you hand me the rubber, Grandad?"

→ **tirer un coup** = to fire a shot; *(in slang)* = to get laid; **douille** = cartridge case; **couille** = testicle

■ Penis Envy

Un petit garçon, dans une cour d'école, demande à son copain, Roger:
- Eh, t'habites à combien de kilomètres de Tours?
- Je sais pas, dit l'autre. 100 ou 200.
Le petit garçon hurle de rire et apostrophe ses amis:
- Eh, les gars! Y'a Roger qui a dit que sa bite avait 200 kilomètres de tour!
Le jeune Roger, comprenant qu'il s'est fait avoir, va voir un autre camarade:
- Eh, Martin. T'habites à combien de kilomètres de Bordeaux?

A schoolboy is in the playground during break. He asks his friend Roger:
- "Hey Roger, how many kilometres do you live from Tours?"
- "I don't know", Roger says. "One or two hundred kilometres."
The schoolboy bursts out laughing:
- "Hey guys! Roger's just told me that his dick is 200 kilometres round!"
Roger understands that he's been made a fool of and he wants to get his own back, so he walks up to another boy and asks him:
- "Hey Martin, how many kilometres do you live from Bordeaux?"

→ **t'habites à combien de kilomètres de Tours** = how many kilometres do you live from Tours?; **ta bite a combien de kilomètres de tour** = what is the girth of your penis?

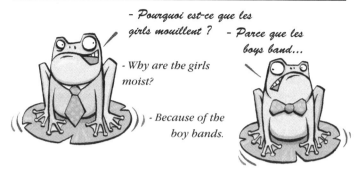

- *Pourquoi est-ce que les girls mouillent ?*
- *Why are the girls moist?*
- *Because of the boy bands.*
- *Parce que les boys band...*

→ **les girls mouillent** = the girls are moist; **les boys band** = pun on "les boys bandent" = the boys are randy

■ Hero worship

Un admirateur se présente chez Jean Cocteau. Le valet de chambre ouvre la porte:
- C'est pour le maître?
- Non! C'est pour le voir...

An admirer of Jean Cocteau turns up at his house. The butler answers the door:
- *"Are you here for the Master?"*
- *"No, I'd just like to see him..."*

→ **le maître** = the master; **le mettre** *(in slang)* = to sodomize him; Jean Cocteau, poet, writer and film-maker, never attempted to hide his homosexuality

■ Cherry picking, rude style

Un paysan embauche du personnel pour faire la cueillette des cerises. Il donne les instructions à une nouvelle recrue:
- Vous voyez cette rangée? Il faut me cueillir toutes les cerises qui sont dans cette rangée.
Le jeune homme s'y met, mais apparemment, il ne se débrouille pas très bien. Au bout d'un panier, le paysan lui dit:
- Les cerises, c'est pas comme ça qu'il faut les cueillir, voyons!! Faut les cueillir avec la queue!
Et l'autre lui répond:
- Vous savez, j'ai déjà beaucoup de mal avec les mains...

A farmer is hiring labourers to pick cherries. He is giving
instructions to a new recruit:
- "You see this row of trees? Well, you've got to pick all the cherries
in this row."
The young man gets busy but he's not very good at it. After a
while, the farmer tells him:
- "That's not the way to pick cherries, young man! Come on!
You've got to pick them with the stalk!"
And the young man replies:
- "You know, I find it difficult enough as it is picking them with
my hands."

→ **la queue** = the stalk; *(in slang)* = the penis

■ Of Mice and Men

Une petite souris se promène à la campagne et arrive à une voie
ferrée. Elle la traverse mais, malheureusement, elle est un peu
lente: un train passe et lui coupe un bout de queue. Alors la petite
souris se dit: "il faut que j'aille récupérer mon bout de queue,
quand même." Elle retourne récupérer son bout de queue et là, il
y a un deuxième train qui passe et qui lui coupe la tête.
Moralité: il n'est pas rare de voir les souris perdre la tête pour un
petit bout de queue.

A little mouse is going for a walk in the countryside and gets to a
railway track. It starts to cross it, quite slowly, too slowly: a train
comes along and the mouse gets the tip of its tail cut off.
"I have to get the tip of my tail back", thinks the mouse once it's
made it to the other side. So it retraces its steps, but just as it gets
to the track, another train comes along and cuts off the little
mouse's head. The moral of the story is that it is not uncommon
for mice to lose their heads over a little bit of tail.

→ **une souris** = a mouse; *(in slang)* = a woman; **la queue** = the
tail; *(in slang)* = the penis

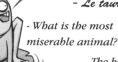

- *Quel est l'animal le plus malheureux??*

- *Le taureau, parce que sa femme est vache.*

- *What is the most miserable animal?*

- *The bull, because his wife is such a cow.*

■ You're never too old to get screwed

Une vieille rombière demande à un chauffeur de taxi d'une ville inconnue s'il connaît une adresse où elle pourrait se faire baiser. Le chauffeur la conduit jusqu'à une maison dont la porte est munie d'un petit judas.

Elle frappe, le judas s'ouvre et une voix lui demande ce qu'elle veut.

- Je veux me faire baiser, dit la vieille.

- Parfait, mais c'est un club privé, ici, il faut glisser un billet de 100 euros pour couvrir les frais d'admission.

- Voilà!

Dix minutes passent, la vieille est toujours devant la porte à attendre qu'elle s'ouvre. Elle refrappe à la porte, le judas s'ouvre:

- Oui ?

- Je voudrais me faire baiser !

- Encore?

An old lady gets into a taxi, tells the driver that she's new to the city and asks him if he knows a place where she could get screwed. The taxi driver drops her off in front of a house where the front door is equipped with a peephole.

She knocks, and from the other side of the door a voice asks her what she wants.

- *"I want to get screwed", says the old lady.*

- *"OK, but this is a private club and the admission fee is 100 euros."*

- *"There you are", says the old lady as she slips a 100-euro note through the peephole.*

Ten minutes go by and the old lady is still waiting to be let in. She knocks at the door again and the same person comes to the peephole:

- *"Yes?"*

- *"I would like to get screwed", says the old lady.*

- *"What, again?!", comes the answer.*

→ **se faire baiser** = two different senses in slang: 1/ to have sex 2/ to get ripped off

■ Moaning and groaning

Le médecin examine une femme qui agonise. Il se tourne vers son mari et il lui dit:
- Ça fait longtemps qu'elle râle comme ça?
- Oh, oui! Depuis qu'on est marié.

A doctor is examining a woman who's about to breathe her last, and who's giving the telltale death rattle.
The doctor turns to the husband and asks:
- "How long has she been making this terrible noise?"
- "Er, ever since we got married..."

→ **râler** = to give a death rattle; (in colloquial language) = to grumble

- *Pourquoi les homos attirent toujours les femmes?*

- *Why are women always attracted to gay men?*

- *Parce que les tapettes attirent toujours les souris.*

- *Because mouse-traps always attract mice.*

→ **une tapette** = a mouse-trap; (in slang) = a male homosexual; **une souris** = a mouse; (in slang) = a woman

■ Those wonderful farmyard animals in blue

Le téléphone sonne dans une gendarmerie.
- "Allô?", fait une voix d'homme. "Je viens d'écraser deux poulets en traversant un village. Qu'est-ce que je dois en faire?"
- "Mettez-les sur le bas-côté de la route, pour que les voitures ne leur roulent pas dessus."
- "Et leurs motos, qu'est-ce que j'en fais?"

The phone rings at a police station. A gendarme answers the phone and hears a man's voice at the other end:
- "Hello! I've just run over two pigs while driving through a village. What should I do with them?"
- "Put them at the side of the road so nobody else runs them over."
- "And what should I do with their motorbikes?"

→ **un poulet** = a chicken; *(in slang)* = a policeman

■ Don't get the hump with me!

Un chameau dit à un dromadaire:
- Comment ça va?
- Bien, je bosse, et toi?
- Je bosse, je bosse!

A camel says to a dromedary:
- "How's tricks?"
- "All right, still working; what about you?"
- "Oh, still working, still working!"

→ **une bosse** = a hump; **je bosse** *(in slang)* = I'm working hard; a dromedary has only one hump, a camel has two

■ Old Mrs MacDonald had a farm...

Des frères et sœurs se disputent:
- Quel âne!
- Tête de cochon!
- Espèce de dinde!
Leur mère arrive et crie: "Oh, la ferme!"

Two brothers and their sister are quarrelling:
- *"What an ass!"*
- *"You're so pigheaded!"*
- *"You're such a stupid chick!"*
Their mother arrives and exclaims: "Oh, shut up, you animals!"

→ **la ferme** = the farm; **la ferme!** *(in slang)* = shut up!

■ Thinning on top

- Es-tu coiffeur? demande Julien à son grand-père.
- Non, pourquoi?
- Parce que maman dit que tu frisais la soixantaine, et papa que tu allais nous raser tout l'après-midi.

- "Are you a hairdresser?", young Julian asks his grandfather.
- "No, why do you ask?"
- "Because Mum said that you were almost sixty and Dad said that you were going to bore us all afternoon."

→ **friser** = to curl; **friser la soixantaine** *(in colloquial language)* = to be getting on for sixty; **raser quelqu'un** = to shave someone; *(in slang)* = to bore someone

- Quelle est la différence entre une femme et une clôture?

- What is the difference between a woman and a fence?

- La clôture, on n'a pas besoin de lui dire «je t'aime» avant de la sauter.

- You don't need to tell a fence that you love it before jumping it.

→ **sauter** = to jump over; *(in slang)* = to have sex with

■ Anatomy and geography

La maîtresse dit à Julien:
- Une grande rue s'appelle une artère.
- Ouais, et la traverser sans se faire écraser, c'est une veine!

The schoolteacher tells Julian:
- "A large street is called a thoroughfare."
- "Yes, and crossing one without being run over is a stroke of luck."

→ **une artère** = 1/ an artery 2/ a thoroughfare; **une veine** = a vein
but **c'est une veine** *(in slang)* = that's a stroke of luck

■ Don't bug me!

Un jour un monsieur entre chez un droguiste:
- Bonjour je voudrais un insecticide.
- C'est pour les moustiques ou pour les mites?
- C'est pour moi... J'ai le cafard.

A man walks into a shop:
- "Hello, I would like some insecticide, please."
- "Is it to get rid of mosquitoes? Or moths maybe?"
- "No, it's for me: I feel very depressed."

→ **un cafard** = a cockroach; **avoir le cafard** = to feel depressed

■ Self-employment

Deux potes discutent:
- Pourquoi t'es-tu reconverti de paysan en vitrier?
- C'est à cause de ma femme. Elle voulait plus que je laboure alors
je mastique.

Two friends are talking:
- "Why did you decide to give up farming to become a glazier?"
- "Because of my wife: she didn't want me to plough any more, so now I work with putty."

→ **je laboure** = I'm ploughing the field, but **je la bourre** *(in slang)* = I'm having sex with her; **le mastique** = putty, but **je m'astique** *(in slang, from "astiquer", which means "to polish")* = I'm masturbating

- Pourquoi les vieilles filles sont-elles toujours constipées?

- Why are spinsters always constipated?

- Elles n'ont pas de mari pour les faire chier!

- Because they don't have husbands to bug them.

→ **chier** = to shit; **faire chier quelqu'un** = to annoy someone

■ Family fun and games

J'ai du mal à m'y retrouver parmi les membres de ma famille; pensez donc: mon père est maire, j'ai un cousin qui est frère, mon frère est masseur, ma tante est sœur, et mon oncle est une tante.

Trying to figure out who's who in my family is extremely tricky. Just imagine: my father is a mayor/my mother, I've got a cousin who's a monk/brother, my brother is a masseur/my sister, my aunt is a nun/sister, and my uncle is a poof/an aunt.

→ **mère** = mother; **maire** (same pronunciation as "**mère**") = mayor; **frère** = 1/brother 2/monk; **masseur** (a man who does massage) is pronounced like "**ma sœur**" ("my sister"); **sœur** = 1/ sister 2/ nun; **tante** = aunt; *(in slang)* = male homosexual

■ Did the earth move for you?

Deux amants d'une nuit se quittent au matin:
- Merci, c'était super; tu sais, j'avais encore jamais couché avec une Mexicaine.
- Et moi j'avais encore jamais couché avec un mec si con!

A man and a woman say goodbye after a one-night stand:
- *"Thanks a lot, that was great", says the man. "You know, I've never slept with a Mexican woman before."*
- *"And I've never slept with a jerk like you before!"*

→ **un mec si con** = such a jerk

■ Snookered!

À l'école, la maîtresse demande aux élèves de nommer des animaux velus.
Toto lève le doigt et dit:
- Les boules de billard, Madame!!
- Mais voyons, Toto, d'une part les boules de billard ne sont pas des animaux et d'autre part je n'ai jamais vu le moindre poil sur une boule de billard!
- C'est que vous n'avez pas bien regardé. Hé, Billard, montre tes boules à la maîtresse!

The schoolteacher wants the pupils to name some furry animals. Toto raises his hand and says:
- *"Billiard balls, Miss!"*
- *"Come on, Toto!", says the teacher. "For one thing, billiard balls are not animals, plus I've never seen a hairy one!"*
- *"It's probably because you haven't looked hard enough, Miss... Hey, Billard! Come and show the teacher your balls!"*

→ **des boules de billard** = billiard balls; **les boules de Billard** (Billard being someone's name) = Billard's testicles

■ Career choice: lecher

- Quelle est ta matière préférée à l'école, mon garçon?
- À vrai dire, il y en a deux: math et dessin!

- "What's your favourite subject at school, young man?"
- "Actually, I've got two: maths and art."

→ **math et dessin** = maths and art; **mater des seins** *(in slang)* = to look at breasts

■ Just one Esk-i-mo

Deux Esquimaux à Paris devant un cinéma:
- Dis donc, si on allait là?
- Oh non, on va rien comprendre.
- Oui, mais y paraît qu'on nous suce à l'entracte!

> *Two Eskimos are standing in front of a cinema in Paris:*
> - *"Say, what about going in there?"*
> - *"No way, we won't understand a thing!"*
> - *"Maybe not, but I heard that we get sucked during the inter-mission!"*

→ **un Esquimau** = an Eskimo; **un esquimau** = an ice lolly; **sucer** = to lick; *(in slang)* = to perform oral sex on

■ Sex, politics and the automobile

- Pourquoi est-ce que quand tu parles de ton ami qui est communiste et homosexuel, tu l'appelles l'"embrayage"?
- Parce que c'est la pédale de gauche.

> - *"Why do you call your gay communist friend 'the clutch pedal'?"*
> - *"That's because he's the pedal on the left."*

→ **une pédale** = a pedal; *(in slang)* = a male homosexual; **la pédale de gauche** = the pedal on the left; *(in slang)* = the homosexual leftie; **l'embrayage** = the clutch

■ Love among the wrinklies

Deux anciens amants se retrouvent cinquante ans après leurs derniers ébats.
- Oh! Mon vieux complice! s'écrit la dame.
- Ma bite aussi! répond le monsieur.

> *An old woman and an old man run into each other fifty years after they last slept with each other.*
> - *"Oh! My old companion!" exclaims the lady.*
> - *"So is my dick!" says the old man.*

→ **mon vieux complice** = my old companion; **mon vieux con plisse** *(in slang)* = my old pussy is all wrinkly

*- Pourquoi l'onanisme est-il
si démocratique?*

*- Why is masturbation so
democratic?*

*- Parce qu'il est à la portée de
toutes les bourses.*

*- Because everyone can
afford it.*

→ **une bourse** = a purse, but **les bourses** = the scrotum; **être à la
portée de toutes les bourses** = 1/ to be affordable by everybody
2/ to be close to all scrotums

■ Some more riddles

- Qu'est-ce qui est aussi efficace que le Viagra et qui coûte beaucoup
moins cher?
- De l'eau chaude, car ça fait gonfler les nouilles, durcir les œufs
et ouvrir les moules...

- What is every bit as efficient as Viagra but a lot cheaper?
*- Hot water, because you use it to make noodles swell, to make
hard-boiled eggs, and it also makes mussels open.*

→ **les nouilles** = pasta; *(in slang)* = penises; **les œufs** = eggs; *(in
slang)* = testicles; **les moules** = mussels; *(in slang)* = female
genitals

- Quel est la lettre de l'alphabet qui représente le mieux l'homme?
- Le "Q", parce que c'est un gros zéro avec une petite queue.

Rude French humour

- *Which letter of the alphabet is most like a man?*
- *The letter Q, because it's a zero with a little tail.*

→ **un gros zéro** = a big nought; *(in slang)* = a nonentity; **une queue** = a stem, a tail; *(in slang)* = a penis

- Quelle est la différence entre un intellectuel et un gay?
- Ben, l'intellectuel a le Petit Larousse dans la tête. Et le gay, le gros Robert dans le cul...

- *What is the difference between an intellectual guy and a gay guy?*
- *Well, the intellectual guy has the entire Petit Larousse in his brain, and the gay guy has Big Robert up his arse...*

→ **Le Petit Larousse** = a famous one-volume French dictionary; **le Gros Robert** = big Robert (allusion to **Le Grand Robert**, a French dictionary in several volumes).

- Quelle est la différence entre un homme qui va faire l'amour et un homme qui vient de faire l'amour?
- L'homme qui va faire l'amour a le sang qui bout et l'homme qui vient de faire l'amour a le bout qui sent.

- *What is the difference between a man who is about to have sex and a man who has just had sex?*
- *A man who's about to have sex is excited no end and one who's just had sex has a smelly end.*

→ **avoir le sang qui bout** = to be very excited (literally "to have one's blood boiling"); **avoir le bout qui sent** *(in slang)* = to have a smelly penis

- Quel est le point commun entre un poulet rôti et une belle fille bronzée?
- Dans les deux cas c'est le blanc le meilleur.

- *What have a roast chicken and a beautiful girl with a tan got in common?*
- *In both cases, it's the white bits that are the best.*

→ **le blanc** (of chicken) = the white meat; (of tanned person) = the white bits

- Quelle différence y a-t-il entre un Français et un Anglais qui veulent faire un bon repas?
- Le Français tombe la veste et l'Anglais passe la Manche.

- *What's the difference between a Frenchman and an Englishman getting ready for a good meal?*
- *The Frenchman takes off his jacket and the Englishman crosses the Channel.*

→ **tomber la veste** = to take off one's jacket; **passer la Manche** = to cross the Channel (la manche = the sleeve; **la Manche** = the English Channel)

- Quelle est la différence entre un voleur et un chimpanzé?
- Eh bien, l'un a la police au cul... et l'autre a la peau lisse au cul.

- *What's the difference between a thief and a chimpanzee?*
- *One has the police on his tail and the other has a smooth bottom.*

→ **avoir la police au cul** = to have the police on one's tail; **avoir la peau lisse au cul** = to have a smooth bottom

- Quelle est la différence entre une femme et une chasse d'eau?

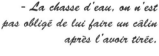

- *What is the difference between a woman and a toilet flush?*

- La chasse d'eau, on n'est pas obligé de lui faire un câlin après l'avoir tirée.

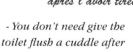

- *You don't need give the toilet flush a cuddle after using it.*

→ **tirer la chasse d'eau** = to flush; **tirer une femme** *(in slang)* = to have sex with a woman

Body Language

In some situations, gestures can express feelings more eloquently than words, no matter how colourful these may be. In fact there are situations in which gestures are the only option. If, for instance, you are sitting at a table with people, one of whom is holding forth about the fact that "Les Bleus" really should have won the World Cup Final of 2006 because "let's face it, they played a better game, and the Italians definitely used dirty tricks, and even though I'm against violence, one can't deny that.... blah blah blah", a discreet "razor" gesture to your friends (when the speaker is not looking) will convey your feelings of boredom to the other listeners while sparing the speaker's feelings. Similarly, the "bras d'honneur" can be understood by people out of earshot of the gesturer and since it is visible from a distance it affords the perpetrator a degree of safety from immediate retribution. So, arm yourself with patience and a mirror, and get practising!

❶ Boredom

This is the gestural equivalent of the expression "c'est rasoir/rasant", meaning "it's boring" (the literal meaning of "rasoir" being "razor"). The back of the hand strokes the cheek in a razor-like gesture and the face bears an expression of utter boredom; a stifled yawn is a good addition to the gesture but is by no means mandatory. It should be noted that, strangely enough, this is not a gender-specific gesture and no one will be surprised if a woman mimics shaving in order to express her boredom.

❷ The Gallic shrug

As its name indicates, the Gallic shrug is often perceived as a quintessentially French piece of body language although some non-French people have also been known to give the occasional shrug. A quick shrug will usually express indifference or lack of enthusiasm (in which case its verbal equivalent is "bof!") and a slow shrug may indicate doubt or uncertainty. Hands can be used for emphasis, but this is entirely at the shrugger's discretion. It is perfectly possible to give a bona fide shrug with one's hands deep in one's pockets. The shrugger's head will often be slightly tilted sideways and the mouth twisted downwards.

❸ Anguish/Irritation

The accompanying gesture to "avoir les glandes/
les boules". This gesture is said to have originated
from the imaginary migration of testicles (or
ovaries) all the way to the lymph glands of the
neck under the effect of deep irritation or anguish.
Others say that the gesture actually mimics
difficulty in swallowing, which is a symptom of
anxiety. In any case, it must be accompanied by
a grimace.

❹ Drunkenness

This gesture is used to allude to someone's (and in certain cases one's own) state of inebriation. It involves grabbing one's nose in one's hand and pretending to twist it in an anticlockwise motion (for right-handers) or a clockwise motion (for left-handers). The origin of the gesture is difficult to ascertain although it is believed that it could be linked to either "en avoir un coup dans le nez" or possibly to "être poivré", both expressions meaning "to be drunk". The latter origin might be slightly more probable than the former considering that its literal meaning is "to be peppered" and that the movement of the hand on the nose greatly resembles the motion of a hand operating a pepper mill.

❺ Weariness

A classic and one of the most basic items of the French gestural lexicon. It is the physical equivalent of the expression "en avoir ras le bol". The edge of one's hand should run across one's forehead in a gesture similar to the one that would accompany "I've had it up to here" in English. Although in French slang the word "bol" originally referred to the posterior and as such the expression used to be related to "en avoir plein le cul", there has been a shift in meaning over time and people now understand the expression as meaning "to have one's bowl full to the brim", where the word "bol" means "the head", hence the gesture. The image here is reminiscent of another expression, namely "la coupe est pleine" ('the cup is full'). At any rate it is a gesture used to express intense weariness, so the person's face should wear an expression of annoyance, disgust or dejection.

❻ Missing out on something

This is the gestural version of the expression "ça m'est passé sous le nez" (literally "it went straight under my nose"). This gesture is the ideal accompaniment to a host of situations having to do with failure, and more specifically failure to obtain something that one was coveting. Place your forefinger horizontally under your nose and move it in a straight line from right to left if you're a right-hander, and from left to right if you're a left-hander. You may want to accompany the gesture with a little whistling noise, as a sound effect to the motion of the hand. This gesture is very versatile and can be used in a wide variety of contexts such as being turned down for a salary rise or a loan, failing a job interview, being passed up for promotion, not getting the 2012 Olympics or failing to get one's oats.

❼ To run off

Imagine that you and your friend have just consumed a dozen "demis" each at the terrace of a Parisian café and you suddenly realize that you've both left your wallets in your hotel room... or maybe you're at a nightclub and the girl that you've both been busy chatting up suddenly insists on introducing you to her boyfriend who also doubles up as the bouncer... Both perfect opportunities to use this gesture which is a discreet invitation to make tracks and yourselves scarce. Directions: place one hand over the wrist of the second hand (obviously!) and simultaneously move the second hand as if indicating the direction "straight ahead", palm vertical with fingers extended. Don't worry if you don't get it right the first time round though, as it is preferable to wait until you've escaped to safety before practising this most useful of gestures.

❽ I don't care

This gesture is used to convey a very strong feeling of indifference. It is the gestural equivalent to "rien à foutre!", which means "I couldn't care less". The palm of your hand should be facing up but your fingers should not be fully extended. Your hand should look somewhat as if it was holding an imaginary ball of crumpled paper. You should then bend your arm as if you were throwing the imaginary ball over your shoulder (of the same arm). So, if you're passionate about your indifference and keen to publicize your couldn't-care-less attitude, this gesture is for you.

❾ Scepticism

This gesture is often used in conjunction with the expression "mon œil!" (which translates as "my eye!" or "my foot!"), and is a way of conveying the fact that you are less than convinced by the supposed veracity of a statement that has just been made by another party. Your forefinger should stretch the skin under your eye (people with sharp nails are invited to exercise caution) in a manner reminiscent of a person asking somebody to inspect his or her eye for a foreign body. This gesture is perfectly acceptable on its own, without any verbal comment on the part of the disbeliever.

⑩ **Blimey!**

This is quite a versatile gesture that can be used in a number of contexts. It is most commonly used when trying to show your surprise or when trying to render the intensity of some experience you've had (such as the pain you suffered in the dentist's chair or your shock at seeing your latest garage bill); alternatively it can be meant as a sympathetic reaction to someone's bad news. It is often accompanied by "la vache!" or "Oh! là! là!" (which, contrary to what many Britons believe, doesn't necessarily have "naughty" connotations). Hold your hand in front of you, palm facing you and fingers loose, and shake it up and down, rather as if you had just burned it or as if you were trying to get rid of a sticky sweet wrapper.

⓪ Le bras d'honneur

A gesture that expresses one's displeasure with somebody else in a very graphic way. Although not everybody is aware of it, the "bras d'honneur" is supposed to symbolize sodomy in much the same way as the middle finger salute in Britain, but in a more brutal fashion. The fist must be firmly clenched and the look on the face menacing. The main problem with this gesture is that it requires both hands; when driving or operating heavy machinery the "doigt d'honneur" (what Americans call the "bird" and British people the "finger", as mentioned above) is preferable.

Contrepèteries/ Spoonerisms

Le Petit Robert gives the following definition for *contrepèterie*: "interversion des lettres ou des syllabes d'un ensemble de mots spécialement choisis, afin d'en obtenir d'autres dont l'assemblage ait également un sens, de préférence burlesque ou grivois" (the deliberate switching of letters or syllables of a series of words to create new words with a different, often crude meaning); this is a definition which more or less applies to the English word "spoonerism" except for the fact that "spoonerism" usually refers to the accidental transposition of sounds between words in English, whereas French "contrepèteries" are always deliberate.

Being essentially a polysyllabic language, French is particularly well-suited for this type of verbal game. Indeed, "la contrepèterie" has almost evolved into an art form in its own right, with enthusiasts compiling lists of thousands of them.

In keeping with the overall tone of this book, the ones that we have selected are of the salacious kind (though by no means as salacious as they get), and the vocabulary that you have learnt in the preceding chapters will come in handy as you attempt to solve them.

The letters or syllables that need to be switched around appear in **bold**.

Examples:

"une femme **f**olle de la **m**esse" >> une femme molle de la fesse
"la **b**erge du ** r**avin" >> la verge du rabbin
"**gli**sser dans la **pi**scine" >> pisser dans la glycine

1) La femme du capitaine l'a fait **m**ander à **b**ord.
    The captain's wife had him summoned aboard.

2) Vous trouvez ça **b**eau, Mag**r**itte?
    Do you like Magritte's paintings?

3) Vous avez vu la **m**ine de votre **p**arrain?
   Have you seen the look on your godfather's face?

4) Au Zam**bèze**, les filles sont jolies et gen**tilles**.
   In the Zambezi, the girls are pretty and friendly.

5) Ce jeune homme **d**anse comme un **b**allot.
   This young man is making a fool of himself dancing.

6) J'ai retiré la **cl**ef du **b**ac.
   I removed the key from the tray.

7) Votre **p**ère a l'air **m**utin.
   Your father looks mischievous.

8) Il se fait des **n**ouilles, encore.
   He's cooking some pasta for himself, yet again.

9) Je n'ai pas de re**b**ord à **m**es épaulettes.
   My epaulettes have no trimmings.

10) C'est Di**manche**: un bon coup de **vin**!
    Today's Sunday: let's drink some wine!

Solutions to the spoonerisms

1) La femme du capitaine l'a fait bander à mort. (mander/bord >> bander/mort)
The captain's wife made him very randy.

2) Vous trouvez ça gros, ma bite? (beau/Magritte >> gros/ma bite)
Do you think I've got a large penis?

3) Vous avez vu la pine de votre marin? (mine/parrain >> pine/marin)
Have you seen your sailor's penis?

4) Aux Antilles, les filles sont jolies et j'en baise. (Zambèze/gentilles >> zAntilles (because of the liaison)/j'en baise)
In the West Indies, the girls are pretty and I make love to some of them.

5) Ce jeune homme bande comme un salaud. (danse/ballot >> bande/salaud)
This young man is incredibly randy.

6) J'ai retiré l'abbé du claque. (la clef/du bac >> l'abbé/du claque)
I dragged the abbot away from the brothel.

7) Votre mère a l'air putain. (père/mutin >> mère/putain)
Your mother looks like a slut.

8) Il se fait des couilles en or. (nouilles/encore >> couilles/en or)
He's making money hand over fist.

9) Je n'ai pas de remords à baiser Paulette. (rebords/mes épaulettes >> remords/baiser Paulette)
I don't feel guilty about having sex with Paulette.

10) C'est divin un bon coup de manche! (dimanche/vin >> divin/manche)
A good roll in the hay is just divine.

Answers to the Test your Rude French Quizzes

Rude Accommodation
1.a 2.b 3.c

Rude Drinking
1.b 2.b 3.c

Rude Driving
1.b 2.c 3.c

Rude Families
1.a 2.b 3.c

Rude Feelings
1.a 2.b 3.c

Rude Food
1.b 2.c 3.a

Rude Foreigners
1.c 2.b 3.b

Rude Health
1.a 2.b 3.c

Rude Leisure
1.c 2.c 3.b

Rude Nightclubbing
1.b 2.a 3.b

Rude Policing
1.a 2.b 3.c

Rude Schools
1.b 2.a 3.a

Rude Sex
1.c 2.b 3.c

Rude Shopping
1.c 2.b 3.c

Rude Work
1.b 2.c 3.a